It was years ago I first learned ~~P9-AQA-297~~ *now how intimately involved I would become in both her life and death. Stacey Magargle taught me many lessons, not the least of which is that God is utterly sovereign over the decisions we make. I also learned the painful lesson of learning to think—and think hard—before speaking. I am so glad to now see* A Time to Die, A Time to Live *in print, and I hope as you read that you, too, will learn timeless lessons about life and death, care and compassion, and how we can best support each other through the toughest of times. The book you hold in your hands is a deeply personal look into the heart of Nancy, Stacey's mother. I pray that in these pages, you will see how deep and wide a mother's love will go when faced with impossible choices. And that, perhaps, is the best lesson of all.*

—Joni Eareckson Tada
Joni and Friends International Disability Center

A Time to Die, A Time to Live *is the story of a mother's journey through the deep grief of losing a child. Magargle invites you into an authentic journey of grief that offers insights into the universal search for God in the midst of suffering and loss. She leads you to the very bosom of God, a place each of us longs for, peace in the shelter of His Wings, comfort through a more intimate knowledge of God.*

—Reni Weixler, MA, LPC, CPC
Licensed Professional Counselor

I find Nancy's message compelling reading as a story of her faith, of Stacey's life, of a life-and-death struggle, and of tensions in her life and marriage. Articulate and poignant, she chronicles the dilemmas and the pain that accompanied each significant step. I was drawn into the experience. At almost every turn, it kept me asking, "What happens next?" Thank you, Nancy, for sharing your message—a gift from God that you give to your readers.

—Pastor David Martino
Community Mennonite Fellowship

May 1993, Stacey leaving for her last vocal performance,
Good-bye, My Friend, as part of her high school's Pops
Concert. Music was a large part of her life.

To my husband, who patiently waited for me to come back;

To Chuck and Kit, who showed me The Way;

To my Savior and Lord, whose footsteps led me to the heart of God:

Home at last.

NANCY MAGARGLE

A Time to
Die,
A Time to
Live

Making and Moving Beyond End-of-Life Decisions

To everything there is a season,
and a time to every purpose under the Heaven:
A time to be born, and a time to die.
(Ecclesiastes 3:1–2 AKJV)

Carpenter's Son Publishing

A note to the readers: *the names and identifying details of some of the people and places portrayed in this book have been changed.*

Published by Carpenter's Son Publishing, Franklin, Tennessee

Published in association with Larry Carpenter of Christian Book Services, LLC

www.christianbookservices.com

The views expressed in this work are solely those of the author and do not necessarily reflect the views of the publisher, and the publisher hereby disclaims any responsibility for them.

Bible Translations

All Scripture quotations, unless otherwise indicated, are taken from the New American Standard Bible. Copyright © 1960, 1962, 1963, 1968, 1971, 1972, 1973, 1975, 1977, 1995 by The Lockman Foundation.

Scripture quotations marked AKJV are taken from the American King James Version, a word for word update from the King James English Version. Stone Engelbrite put the American King James version of the Bible into the public domain on November 8, 1999.

Scripture quotations marked AMP are taken from the Amplified® Bible, Copyright © 1954, 1958, 1962, 1964, 1965, 1987 by The Lockman Foundation. Scripture quoted by permission.

Scripture quotations marked CGSB are taken from the Christian Growth Study Bible, New International Version. Copyright ©1997 by The Zondervan Corporation.

Scripture quotations marked ESV are taken from The Holy Bible, English Standard Version. Copyright © 2001 by Crossway Bibles, a division of Good News Publishers.

Scripture quotations marked GWT are taken from God's Word® Translation. Copyright © 2011 by Revell, a division of Baker Publishing Group.

Scripture quotations marked KJV are taken from King James Version of the Bible.

Scripture quotations marked NIV are taken from THE HOLY BIBLE, NEW INTERNATIONAL VERSION®, NIV® Copyright © 1973, 1978, 1984, 2011 by Biblica, Inc.® Used by permission. All rights reserved worldwide.

Scripture quotations marked NKJV are taken from the New King James Version. Copyright © 1979, 1980, 1982, by Thomas Nelson Inc., Publishers.

Scripture quotations marked NLT are taken from the Holy Bible, New Living Translation. Copyright ©1996 by Tyndale House Publishers, Inc.

Editing, illustration, and interior design by Adept Content Solutions

Cover design by Suzanne Lawing

ISBN   978-1-942587-77-4

Printed in the United States of America

CONTENTS

PREFACE Walking Among the Clouds vii

1 For Such a Time as This 1
2 Looking Back and Inching Forward 9
3 Fighting for Life 16
4 Will She Live if You Don't Operate? 21
5 The Nightmare Was Real 31
6 The Illusion of Control Becomes the Idol of Control 39
7 Stubborn Hope 48
8 Who Really Cares about Stacey? 56
9 Greyson, First Report 65
10 Walking in the Light 72
11 The Beginning of the End 77
12 Straining to Find the Path 83
13 David's Oath 91
14 Walking in the Shadows 96
15 Holding On 102
16 Heavenly Provision 107
17 The Shepherd Leads 116
18 The Fleece 125
19 The Pain of Withdrawal 130
20 The Letter 135
21 Saying Goodbye 145
22 The Forks in the Road—My Crisis of Belief 151
23 Satan's Prison, God's Promise 158

24   Mortar for My Prison Walls   165

25   Walking toward Forgiveness   173

26   Finding Myself along the Way   186

27   Rescued by His Love   193

28   Revelations of His Love   200

EPILOGUE   The Pilgrimage—True North to Home   206

RESOURCES   211

ADDENDUM ONE   Medical References   212

ADDENDUM TWO   The Way of Pain   214

ADDENDUM THREE   Revelations of His Love—List   217

ADDENDUM FOUR   Chronology of Stacey's Decline   220

NOTES   222

ACKNOWLEDGMENTS   230

Walking Among the Clouds

Nature provides the parchment upon
which God writes His love lessons.

He is my tutor. I am His student.

Autumn tore more than leaves from trees. It tore my daughter
from my arms. Winter solstice settled into my bones as ice
settles into frozen terra. In the winter of my soul, in the wake of
crippling guilt, devastating loss, and spiritual darkness, I glimpsed
God's glorious Light. Glistening adornment, sent from His heavens,
transformed my dark and wintery mindset into faith's confident expectation.

Amidst grief's dark winter, snow's falling erected a cathedral.
God met me there.

Ancient water floated from heaven, filled the sky, and colored
the world hazy blue. Holy fingers formed puffballs from ageless vapor emptied from frozen clouds hung as high as the stars are fixed.
They drifted down—as manna from the throne room of God and
the Heavenly City—and melted upon my heart. The crystalline water
flakes fell as softly as mourning doves, lighting upon tethered telephone wires to form a skyline of folded feathers aloft. Snow clothed
winter's skeleton, wrapping gun-steeled branches.

I plowed upward through the virgin snow to where stubbled fields
met spruce-firred forest. Breathing heavily and slogging through

snow, sand, water—or life's storms—enlarges the soul. Pausing, breathless, my soul spread to soak up this beauty. The Lord composed a woodland sanctuary, a meeting place where He would sing my soul alive. He made the clouds His chariot, He soared on the wings of the wind, and *now He walked with me* among these iridescent jewels.

Hesitating only a moment, I turned off the main concourse and took a logging trail down, up, and down again through the whistling hollows. I walked on spotless snow-carpet. Nature donned her woolen coverlet. Pines, hemlocks, and evergreens of all sorts held the snow with outstretched arms as one holds a bubble in a wand, aware that only a glancing breeze might spontaneously burst the vitreous liquid or dismantle winter's fluff-fur coat. Snow-draped, the vista rolled before me for miles of unharnessed forested beauty.

As quietly as it had commenced, the hushed snow now suspended. The woods stilled.

It came to me—or me to it. I am not sure who traveled to whom. It hung from high in an oak tree. I might have missed it but that I gazed heavenward. Upon its slender thread lay sparkling snow crystals, only intermittently, barely close enough to decipher the continuous coded-line—thinner than fishing line—fastening frozen ground to leafy branches perched far above my head. I couldn't tell if it climbed higher or ended among the overhanging appendages. I could only barely discern that somewhere, from heaven's heights, the spinner decided to cast a thread of proteinaceous spider silk, a bridge-line. I paused a moment in wonder of spotting such a delicate creation amidst the splattering snow stuck on wood, stubble, stone—all that stood perpendicular to heaven or lay upon earth's floor.

This single strand of silk hung suspended before my face, only inches from me. What wonders fill the earth! I paused, arrested by God's power and presence displayed in His creation, then hurried on, determined to reach the hollow's bottom where water springs freely from earth's bosom. I yearned to hear life flowing through rocky places that day.

Where crystal liquid bubbled from deep and cryptic springs, I stood still. Listening, I breathed in the harmony of the Life-giver's aria, the melody that trickles through every configuration of this world's stony path. Water's melody swelled with grace notes of wings' fluttering, snows' dripping, and leaves' rustling. God's symphony played on—unbroken.

Alas, the spinning earth moved 'round the sun, and time ticked off daylight's fleeting moments. Soon the wood's filtered light would dim. I started home.

Wading through deep snow, winding up the ravine, I paused at the top of one hollow to quiet my heaving chest. *Could it be?* There before me poised that same single strand of the orb-weaver. I stood, face to face with the diamond-studded strand of fiber.

How could it be? I recognize nothing to mark this place along my path. Every marker to me is hidden.

Motionless, I waited. Would the silken string come closer? Was it hovering, as a hummingbird over nectar's sweetness? Would the breeze catch it? Would *it* come to *me?* A palm's width from my nose, could my breath draw it nearer or blow it farther from me? I held my breath; it floated across my face, its drift barely perceptible. I tried to breathe it in. It controlled the course; I didn't. I couldn't command its presence nor alter its distance from me. This vertical trail to heaven appeared delicate, yet it was so strong life's storms couldn't break it. I marveled again—the web path discernible solely because of the snow clinging to the thread in spurts. Intermittently, the filament disappeared like a dotted line upon a translucent piece of aerial parchment or the alternating, deliberate on-off code of some celestial messenger.

What hidden communication, what grace-gift had God encoded upon this receptacle now mysteriously hanging unopened before me? What message? Forehead and brow wrinkled and eyes fixed upon the dotted line, I saw it!

I saw it. The web mirrored my perception of God's presence in my life. Intermittent. Sporadic. Here, now—I am fully aware of His presence. Other times—unaware—He felt painfully absent. Had I simply lost sight of Him? And my daughter, my precious child … Stacey had crossed that great chasm fixed between the living and the dead (Luke 16:2).

Stacey reached the "heavenly country."[1] Now she lived with myriads of angels, cherubim, and saints—those who've gone before and now abide in His visible presence in a way in which we earth-dwellers cannot. Yet, because of Christ, although there is an inconceivable distance between heaven and earth, "there is not an impassable gulf, as there is between heaven and hell. This firmament is not a wall of partition, but a way of intercourse."[2]

I couldn't bring Stacey back to life. Nor could I fully live until I moved beyond this dark winter of my soul. As a father cups his child's chin and gently redirects her downward gaze to meet His loving eyes, God directed my gaze heavenward. God the Father showed me through a slender, snow-splattered thread of spider silk: He had been with me all along. Faithful. Constant. He connected all the dots of my life.

My troubled heart stilled. God's aria flowed rhythmically between the visible and the invisible, communicating a message of hope, encouraging me to keep on persevering in my faith. I fixed my heart upon God and vowed to set aside all obstacles in my relationship with Him and with others. I walked on with joy, knowing that although "The earth shall soon dissolve like snow, the sun forbear to shine. But God, who called me here below will be forever mine."[3]

I was, for a time, a prisoner of my own self-imposed guilt and punishment. I was, for a time, a pilgrim, freed, but not living in the reality of freedom in Christ. I invite you to travel this path with me as you turn these pages. I implore you to call out to Jesus and meet with Him along the way. Experience the hope of His promises and the truth of who you *are* and who you *can be* in Christ. I pray that God's perfect love will cast out every fear so you can walk into your future knowing that, "after you have suffered a little while, the God of all grace, who hath called us unto His eternal glory by Christ Jesus, [will] make you perfect, establish, strengthen, [and] settle you" (I Peter 5:10, AKJV).

Beloved, as we journey together, may His sweet fellowship abide with you and impart to you great joy. Will you walk with me into the Light of His perfect Love?

CHAPTER 1

For Such a Time as This

Take comfort that He is in charge,
even when things seem out of control.[4]

(Christian Growth Study Bible, NIV)

For a long time I was unaware of the slithering phantoms, slowly circling, coiling, constricting. Fear paralyzed. Guilt stretched its jaws and swallowed me whole. *God gave her life. I had no right. He meant for me to protect her. I failed.* Life careened out of my control, exposing the cracks in my facade, and forever redefining who I am.

———

Her eyes were mirrors.

The reflection of my own determination startled me—like when you look down into a sunlit creek bottom at the crayfish below and realize they're hiding in the shadow of your own mirrored image. I blinked. I saw my own longing for the other to understand my excitement, my anticipation, and yes, my uneasiness with her leaving us.

Why can't she see the importance of this trip—not just to me but to our whole family? "Come on, Stacey. Maybe Dad will take us on one of those ships again—you know, the ones that weave through the islands. Oh, remember how beautiful they were? How much fun we had? Won't you change your mind? Please, come with us.

"No, Mom. I'm staying home this time."

"But, we've never left any of you behind. It doesn't feel right. With you leaving for college, this might be our last family vacation."

"Mom, Heather will stay with me. We'll have fun planning and packing."

Stacey, our eighteen-year-old daughter and her best friend, Heather, both looked forward to their move to Indiana University of Pennsylvania. They'd finally be out on their own. Stacey couldn't wait to begin college life and to study neonatal nursing. While she anticipated caring for babies, I struggled to let go of my mothering instinct.

"I can help you with all that when we get home. You know we're taking the Jet Ski, Stace. Don't you think ... ? Please come."

"No, Mom. I want to say goodbye to my friends and to work my last week at Friendly's, too."

Wow, she's stubborn! I stewed. *If only her dad would speak up. Maybe he could talk her into coming with us.* I looked into her big brown eyes and took a long, deep breath. I wanted to hold her tight until she gave in. *I must begin to let go of her.*

I didn't want this discussion to escalate into a war, and I certainly didn't want my husband, Ronnie, to hear us fighting about it, so I dropped the subject. It would've been nice to have some kind of backup from her father—this time among many others. He rarely got involved in the bantering between us or between Stacey and her brothers, although he complained often of the ruckus. Earlier this summer, Ronnie and Stacey had locked horns when she took off for Pittsburgh with a friend without telling us.

I usually positioned myself in the middle and tried to keep the peace.

During our drive from Pennsylvania to Canada, I complained to Ronnie about Stacey's absence. "Did you tell Stacey you wanted her to come along? Maybe she would have changed her mind."

"She knows she didn't have to work at the restaurant. I would have given her the money she needs," he said.

"Did you tell her that? Did you even try?"

"You know she's bullheaded. She does what she wants to do."

I wondered if I could've said something more. Could I have convinced her to come with us, or would I only have pushed her farther away?

I missed Stacey. I called each evening to touch base with her.

"Hi, sweetheart. How's it going?"

"We're fine, Mom. Nothing new here. Pappy came up, and Aunt Bonny called to see if we needed anything. They checked on us. I suppose you asked them to."

"Now, Stace, you know Pappy and Aunt Bonny just care about you. I never need to ask either of them to watch over any of us." We both chuckled. "Okay. Well, we love you, honey. I'll see you in a few days, and we'll get you moved into your dorm."

"Love you, too, Mom."

It was good to hear her voice.

Each morning of our vacation, Ronnie and our two sons, fifteen-year-old Casey and twenty-two year-old Rex, left to fish long before daylight. Our seven-year-old daughter, Laura, and I spent those early mornings reading the Book of Esther.

The third morning, Laura and I sat on a quaint little Canadian dock overlooking the Thousand Islands. At that point, Ontario and the United States converge in the mighty waters of the Saint Lawrence River and Lake Ontario. The native peoples called this region, "The Garden of the Great Spirit." The forest merges with the water's edge, creating a perfect vacation environment: calm panoramic vistas of spectacular beauty; fresh, clean air to breathe; and quiet space for spiritual renewal.

The placid water lapped peacefully against the weathered wood. The morning air warmed us as the sun peeked through the fading shadows of night, dispersing the clouds into a full-colored kaleidoscope of translucent reflections on the glassy surface.

At daylight's first glimmer, I opened my Bible and began to read. I welcomed this time away from the demands of everyday life. The Old Testament story of Esther fascinated me. I wanted to learn more about the beautiful, young slave, who became queen through a series of events only an all-knowing, sovereign God could orchestrate.

Confronted with a crisis, Esther learned God truly does intervene in the lives of His people when they respond in faith and obedience to Him, even when facing an unknown and potentially perilous outcome. As Esther trusted Him in the midst of tragic events, God brought about the redemption of her people. Esther's story reminded me God always accomplishes His purposes, one way or another. What He intends, He will carry out.

One of the commentaries I had read that morning posed a thought-provoking question:

> Even as God raised up Esther 'for such a time as this' (Esther 4:14, CGSB) to help save her people, consider why God has allowed *you* to be alive today. What redemptive acts does He want to accomplish through *you*? Take comfort that He is in charge, even when things seem out of control.[5]

I couldn't see beneath the river's tranquil surface, through the clouded water to the frenzy of activity in the depths below. I couldn't see beyond this moment's stillness to the life-altering events soon to strike the ordinary lives of our family and friends like a boulder crashing upon this smooth seaway's surface, creating a wake that would forever redefine us. Oblivious to any of this, yet trusting that God was in charge of my life in all of it and over all of it, I closed my Bible and bowed my head. *Lord, what purpose do You want to accomplish through me?*

Soon Ronnie and the boys returned for us, and we headed back to the cabin. We anticipated a leisurely afternoon of fishing, relaxing, and floating by the peaceful islands dotting the river. However, when we arrived, we found a note on the door instructing us to come to the office. The manager gave Ronnie an emergency message and phone number. He came back to the truck and told us he had spoken with a hospital chaplain.

"Stacey's been in an accident. We need to get back. The chaplain says it doesn't look good. I told her we're at least eight hours away. It's going to take us a while."

"What? What happened? Who did you talk to?"

"Just pack up. We need to leave. Now!"

"Okay. Okay. We need to put Stacey in God's hands."

My husband shrugged and hurried on.

After we loaded the boat onto the trailer, we raced back to the cabin. Still shaken, I walked around in a daze, emptied drawers, cleared shelves, frantically packed away all remnants of our family's vacation, and threw everything into the truck.

What's going on, Lord? Ronnie's really upset this time. Did Stacey total the car? That's it. No it can't be the car. She's really hurt.

The more I packed away our stuff, the more unraveled I became. *He would have told me if she'd been hurt, really hurt, right? He's just mad. Or maybe—.*

Leaving behind the tranquility of picturesque scenery, we started the journey back to Pennsylvania, back to our oldest daughter. Ronnie, Laura, and I rode together in our truck and took the boat. Rex took Casey with him and followed us, pulling the Jet Ski behind his own truck. Around 12:30 p.m., we began to inch our way back to Stacey.

Throughout all those agonizing hours of travel, I feared impending tragedy. *I don't know what's happening to Stacey, Lord. I only know I need to be with her! I need to take care of her. Lord, please take care of her.*

Thankfully, Ronnie drove. He looked straight ahead, entirely focused on getting back. He remained silent. I fervently prayed, uninterrupted. The stoic expression on his face reflected the gravity of the situation. After twenty-one years of marriage, I knew my questions only irritated him. I welcomed the silence, the time and space, to muster all my energy and will.

Few words passed between any of us throughout the grueling

trip home. Although still unaware of the degree of Stacey's injuries, I sensed an overwhelming need to pray she would live. My stomach lurched as I began my unceasing repetition of gut-wrenching pleas to God.

I willed her to breathe in rhythm with me: *Breathe in. Breathe out. Breathe, Stacey, just keep breathing.*

I inhaled and exhaled my silent prayer like someone coaching a woman birthing new life—only this coaching was a desperate effort to *sustain* my daughter's life. Cocooned within the deafening silence of our car, acutely aware of my own breathing, I felt my lungs expand and contract. I mutely screamed out my appeals to God and to Stacey. I ached to breathe life into her.

Lord, please take care of anyone else involved in this accident.

All you need to do is breathe, Baby Doll. Just breathe. I'll be there soon.

It's uncanny how, in our minds, when danger threatens their safety, our children become babies again, no matter what age. *O Lord, this is my baby. I carried her inside me. She suckled at my breast. How I wish I still carried her safe within me. It just can't be her time yet.*

Hold on, Stace. We're coming.

Hours later, we stopped for fuel. Ronnie went inside to pay the bill and hurried back to the car. He finally revealed, "She's still in surgery."

"What? Surgery? 'Still in surgery?'" The volume of my voice increased with each question.

"Who did you talk to?" I pleaded.

"The chaplain at Hobson."

"Hobson? Why's she at Hobson?"

"They life-flighted her to Hobson Medical Center," Ronnie yelled.

"But Hobson's three more hours away!" I persisted, "Why wasn't she taken to Greyson?" Greyson Medical Center is only thirty minutes from our home. It's one of the finest hospitals in Pennsylvania. I didn't expect an explanation from Ronnie. Still, I had hoped for some response.

This is maddening! Lord, will we ever get to Stacey? My baby's in surgery? It took me a moment to take in what I was hearing.

God was silent. Ronnie offered no further information. It didn't matter. *Please, Lord, give the doctors, the nurses, anyone, everyone involved with Stacey's care Your knowledge. Give them Your wisdom and Your understanding of Stacey's injuries and what she needs.*

We continued to inch closer. Each mile marker seemed to crawl by. The air felt thicker than quicksand. I knew my husband was pushing the limit—maybe even speeding—but it seemed endless. I thought we would never get to our daughter.

About six hours into the journey, Ronnie pulled the truck over to the side of the road and got out.

"What's going on now? Why are you stopping?"

"Something's wrong." One of the tires on the trailer had blown out. Rather than take the time to attend to the flat, Ronnie unhitched the trailer from the truck and drove off.

He's leaving the boat behind? Oh, Lord, what isn't he telling me?

Our little girl needed us, and we were still hours away. I wanted to keep driving straight through to Hobson, but Ronnie wanted to stop at our house first.

"Really? Do we really need to go home before we get to Stacey?"

"Yes." he said. "Rex and Casey can follow us home, drop off the Jet Ski, and go back for the boat. You take Laura to Grammy and Pappy's house. She can spend the night with them."

When we finally arrived home, I threw our stuff off the truck onto the driveway. I wanted to grab Ronnie by the neck and lug him back into the truck or maybe shove him across the seat and take over at the wheel. Finally, Ronnie came back, and we took off again.

After ten tortuous hours, we pulled into the hospital parking lot. I spotted my oldest brother, Drexel, standing outside. His presence there—at that time of night—unnerved me. Then I noticed Ronnie's sister waiting with her children near the emergency entrance. *Stacey must really be hurt.*

Next, I saw other family members—some who lived a couple of hours from Hobson. The parking lot lights cast ominous shadows over them as they rushed from inside the hospital to meet us. I struggled to steady my steps, my feet feeling as if encased in cement. As we approached the emergency room entrance, I realized my brothers and sisters who lived even farther away were waiting just inside the door. And there, with more of Ronnie's family, were my closest friends, Stacey's best friend, Heather, and her mother.

I hurried through the hospital entrance. Their faces told a grim tale of painfully long hours waiting for the outcome of surgery.

Oh God. Why are they all here? Oh, my Lord. We're too late.

Coping Strategies

- Call out to God: He's listening. Even if you've never prayed before, what do you have to lose?

- Take comfort: Even when life seems out of control, God is in charge.

CHAPTER 2

Looking Back and Inching Forward

But not a single sparrow can fall to the ground
without your Father knowing it.

(Matthew 10:29, NLT)

Memories once forgotten now surge: Six-year-old Stacey, her brother Rex, and cousin Shawn climbed the old apple tree at the bottom of the cow hollow where we often played.

I heard her sobs. The half-husked ear of corn dropped from my hand and splattered milk everywhere as I ran out to meet them. On the front porch, Rex and Shawn stood with Stacey between them. Blood dripped from her head down her back. Each boy cupped a skinny elbow in his hands as they gingerly helped her up the step. They treated Stacey like a china cup, broken. All three of the little rascals were shook up. Her crying quieted to a whimper when I wrapped her in my arms. I whisked her into the shower. The warm water washed through her blood-matted hair. My eyes strained, fingers searched. Was it just a superficial wound or something more serious?

The shower floor turned red then gradually faded to pink as the water washed over her wound. The amount of blood alarmed me. Yet, I knew injuries to the head bleed more profusely than other parts of the body. After I got a good look and applied pressure for a few minutes, the bleeding stopped. Her stubborn little cowlick, which she detested, stood again defiantly—and so did she. She was ready to go back at it, to conquer that craggy old apple tree.

I called the doctor to see if I should take Stacey in. After looking into her beautiful brown eyes to see if the pupils were the same size, I laid her trembling body on the couch and watched for nausea or vomiting. She settled, mesmerized by *Scooby Doo* and *Sesame Street*. Stacey giggled when she beat her big brother, Shawn, and me at Candy Land. We played with Stacey and kept her awake the entire day as the doctor instructed. Life on Magargle hill went on. Crisis averted.

I took care of Stacey the day she fell from the apple tree with relative ease. I remember singing to the creaking rhythm of my grandmother's rocking chair as I held her and caressed her silky hair. She calmed right down. Stacey loved music.

At four or five years old, just a wee little tyke, she sang for the first time to an audience. Her pretty voice resonated with a sweet timbre when she and her brothers performed for the vesper services at a local fair. All three of our older children sang at church and in nursing homes. The residents couldn't get enough of them.

At six, baptized in a little Baptist church, Stacey's love for the Lord began at an early age. A few years later, we attended a small home church. Pastor Hoffman's exegesis of Scripture was direct, precise, and matter-of-fact, leaving little wiggle room for those on the fence. Stacey most likely accepted the Lord as her Savior during these spiritually nurturing years. In the back of her Bible, she kept notes about all her Sunday school lessons with underlined and highlighted Scriptures throughout the text.

At eight years, Stacey fell off the pony Pappy Magargle gave her but immediately jumped right back on. There were no tears, just a stubborn determination the horse would not get the upper hand on her again. He didn't.

Soon she was climbing to the top of the pyramid on her cheerleading squad. She joined midget cheerleading in elementary school. It provided the perfect outlet for her enthusiasm and energy. She detested exercise but loved cheerleading. We who knew her best chuckled at the irony.

The children performed little skits I wrote as part of my work with the Woman's Christian Temperance Union (WCTU). Each summer, the organization sponsored a summer camp for young people. Stacey eventually became a camp counselor, mentoring the younger children.

Ronnie bought Stacey a little 50 CC Honda scooter so small her feet touched the ground. The boys each got bigger and faster dirt bikes of their own. She rode the "red-seated wonder" all over the farm. Her friends hopped on the back—all without helmets—and off they'd go, grinning from ear to ear. Stacey even gave her little sister a few rides on the scooter before it hit the dusty trail for the last time on Magargle hill, eventually sold to one of the neighbors.

When Stacey put her mind to it, she could tackle anything. Her spirited personality came out at the most ridiculous times and in some unusual ways. Every Christmas Grammy and Pappy Magargle's tree nearly disappeared under a deluge of presents. When Stacey was ten, her teenage cousins Daren and Lonnie hid all of her gifts. Confiscating them from the "family pile," they slipped them farther back under the tree. They continued handing out presents, and Stacey noticed she wasn't getting any to open. After all of the presents were delivered, her stash of presents were "discovered," and she seemed relieved Santa had not forgotten her.

One year later, Lonnie again handed out presents. This time, he noticed there wasn't anything with his name on it. The only gift under the tree for him? A bag of coal. "Dear Lonnie, Santa checked his list, he checked it twice. You came up naughty instead of nice. From Stacey." Almost thirty years later, Lonnie still has the little bag of coal, which has become a family tradition to display every Christmas.

Music became Stacey's passion. She and I sang together in a community choral group. Those nights away from the normal household, just the two of us, helped me get to know Stacey and come to appreciate her as a person apart from my other children. Our mutual love for music became a bond, buffering the transition from adolescence to womanhood.

Our house resounded with music as she practiced piano, voice, and flute—at the piano in our living room, behind her closed bedroom door, and joining in with the car radio. I knew God had gifted her, which brought me great joy.

As a member of the middle-school band and chorus, her voice matured, and she eventually studied under a university music professor. In high school, Stacey auditioned for and performed in show choir and district chorus. She led vocal warm-ups for the entire choir in both middle and high school. Sitting at the grand piano in the auditorium, she played scale-to-scale, going up an octave at a time.

Chosen as a student conductor, Stacey proudly led the choir in performing "This is the Day of the Lord. Let Us Rejoice and Be Glad in It." Two decades later, Amie, a fellow choir member, reminisced, "The song had a tricky time signature—funny how I remember that! We really enjoyed rehearsing for the school musicals. I never attended district chorus with Stacey. She was always better than me."

Only two weeks before graduation, Stacey and three friends (including Amie) sang a beautiful rendition of "Leavin' on a Jet Plane." The girls, decked out in hippie clothes, wore flower garlands I made for their hair. The crowd applauded. I beamed. Stacey wowed the crowd with her solo "Good-bye, My Friend."

Would Stacey ever perform again? Or would we soon say goodbye to our darling daughter?

———

My children grew up around campfires in our backyard, eating s'mores and roasting hotdogs. Rex, Stacey, Casey, and their many friends loved building bonfires in Sneaky Hollow just below our house. They listened to their music booming from their car radios while relaxing and hanging out in that little patch of woods. Stacey's girlfriends often slept over, filling our home with stories of their escapades.

She continued to attend church and youth group events, read her Bible, and meditate on its truths, ultimately telling others of her faith.

As Stacey matured, she struggled for independence. Involved in many things, she always worked hard at whatever she undertook. After her school day, she waitressed until closing several nights a week at a local restaurant. The stress of working and the pressure of choosing a college weighed heavily on her.

Strong will and determination helped Stacey achieve her goals. In school, her hard work and diligence paid off. Having achieved status as an honor student, the neonatal nursing program at Indiana University of Pennsylvania readily accepted her.

Her stubbornness often put her at odds with her father when her choices opposed him. This part of her personality peaked when she became a teenager. It seemed out of character the summer of the accident when, at the last minute, to my surprise and chagrin, she backed out of her responsibility at camp.

Throughout her senior year, Stacey gave Casey a ride to middle school. He thought this "was really cool because most seniors wouldn't give a ride to their little brothers every day and have them accepted by their friends." After the accident, Casey expressed his regret that they had not had more time together. "She just started getting normal again, you know, from all those hormones."

During my fourth pregnancy, Stacey had the entire family praying for a sister. They felt God answered their prayers when Laura arrived. Stacey took on the role as Laura's "little mother." She and her boyfriend, Jesse, even took her along on dates.

"Mom, Laura and I are going down to the restaurant to pick up my paycheck. Can Jesse and I take her to a movie with us later?"

Stacey and Heather delighted in shopping for Laura. The girls often brought home new Barbie dolls and pretty outfits for Laura. They dressed her as sweet as could be, like a baby doll. They also loved to videotape Laura. One of their most entertaining recording sessions consisted of Laura singing *Little Mermaid* songs in the bathtub.

Laura had enough. "Stop taping me!" she squealed. "Mommy, make them quit."

We all laughed at our little mermaid, swishing around in the bubbles. I believe Laura enjoyed playing the part as much as the girls loved capturing her on video.

Stacey loved children, and they adored her. She lavished her affection on many children.

I have four brothers and three sisters. Together with all the spouses, children, and miscellaneous friends, there were nearly thirty of us when we all got together for our annual week in the Pocono Mountains. Stacey looked forward to those summer vacations, especially relishing the late-night chilly dips in the lake and the cozy campfires afterward. She sang the silly campfire songs at the top of her lungs. We all did.

During summer vacation of 1993 at the mountain house, we had all laughed hysterically as Stacey relentlessly begged her little sister and cousin Christine to push her around the lake on a raft. "Come on you two. Play motorboat with me."

The picture of Laura and Chrissy pushing Stacey around while making motor sounds and blowing bubbles in the water would be indelibly imprinted in the memory of each of us.

Stacey had been full of life all summer. Excited about leaving for school, we crammed in so much activity, the weeks raced by. While the guys chose the perfect fishing lures and outfitted the boat for the vacation in Canada, we girls prepared Stacey to begin the next chapter of her life: college. We squeezed in lots of fun trips, shopping for furnishings for her dorm room, new clothes, luggage, and other *essentials*—even some notebooks and pens.

Throughout the summer, I organized the WCTU camp while Stacey worked as many hours as possible at the restaurant. She made new friends while working with Heather, Heather's boyfriend, Bob, and another friend from high school, Aaron. Through Aaron and Bob, Stacey met a young man, Marcus.

After a couple of dates and about two weeks before her accident, Marcus dropped by for Stacey, staying only long enough for her to introduce him to me. To the best of my knowledge, Ronnie never met Marcus. Heather told me Stacey and Marcus hit it off right away. He seemed like a nice young man, but I never had a chance to get to know him.

On August 25, 1993, like lightning bolts from the deepest, darkest sky, these memories struck and reignited the fire within—the current of life flowing through me, the life I prayed still flowed through my daughter.

Coping Strategies

- Embrace memories. Reflect on happier times.

- Make it personal: Display a few personal belongings of your loved one in the hospital room. This will give staff an idea of who this person is and what he or she means to family and friends. Examples are a recent photograph, a favorite CD, or even a baseball mitt.

CHAPTER 3

Fighting
for Life

I was the attending physician. I called the shots.

Dr. Kline

I have very little personal knowledge of what transpired at home while we were in Canada or what happened to Stacey in those first hours after the accident. What I do know I pieced together from family, Stacey's friends, newspaper articles, medical reports, and a report we received requiring our signature for legal matters surrounding the accident. These pieces became the roadmap through this journey.

Sometime after Ronnie and I finally arrived at the hospital, Heather told us Stacey had decided to take off work the day of the accident. Marcus wanted Stacey to meet his mother, who lived about two hours south of us.

She and Marcus left from our house early in the morning in his grey Chevy Cavalier. About one-and-one-half hours into the trip, driving at a high speed, Marcus lost control of the car, which then passed under a tractor-trailer traveling in the opposite direction. The impact of the accident compressed Stacey's body into a little ball under the car's dashboard and forced the car's engine onto Marcus's lap,

16

crushing his legs. I never learned the full extent of his injuries but later found out he did survive the accident.

The police report noted Stacey didn't have her seat belt buckled. *Why not?* A staunch advocate of safety belts, she had even written a school report on the importance of wearing them. I sometimes wonder if a seatbelt might have saved her life.

Fifteen years after the accident, I went back and personally interviewed the two doctors in charge of Stacey's care and recorded their comments. I don't know what I would've done without those recordings when I began to write this memoir. I replayed bits of the recordings a few words at a time. Hunched over my computer, huddled in my home office, I struggled to understand the medical terms. I searched the Internet, scoured medical journals, and read the doctors' notes from day one to the end. From the doctors and other emergency personnel, I learned what took place in the first hours after her accident.

I cried out to God for help to process the information, to understand what had happened to our daughter. Once I began to grasp the gravity of her injuries, I wept until I had no tears left. Finally, I began to comprehend what the doctors had told me.

When first-responders arrived at the site of the accident, they found Stacey in cardiac arrest, unconscious, unresponsive, with no breathing or abnormal breathing. According to the records, they resuscitated her several times, valiantly trying to manually preserve intact brain function until further measures could be taken to restore spontaneous blood circulation and breathing. They immediately started intravenous fluids, oxygen, and blood pressure support while working quickly to protect her airway and to clear her lungs. After inserting the tube into Stacey's lungs, they placed her on a ventilator so she could breathe. Next, they assessed her circulatory system, her blood pressure, and her heart rate. Airway, breathing, circulation—the ABCs of resuscitation. Resuscitation continued until life-flight reached the hospital. The doctors told me they resuscitated her again during surgery.

As Stacey lay on an emergency room gurney, staff from many departments joined the whirl of activity constituting her care—ER nurses, anesthesiologists, radiologists, neurosurgeons, and others. A whole entourage of medical specialists battled to save her life.

Stacey's head wound continued to bleed from her open skull, interrupting critically needed blood supply to her brain. Damaged, the normal sponge-like consistency of Stacey's brain changed, becoming more and more liquid. Within minutes, the tissue decomposed into a mush-like substance and seeped out from the gash on her head. This necrotic brain tissue (nonviable brain tissue) indicated deeper injury to the brain.

The hospital needed permission to operate. They tried several telephone book listings of Magargle and finally reached Pappy Magargle, the first to hear of Stacey's accident. Pappy asked Heather, still at our house, how to reach us. Heather gave Pappy the number to reach us in Canada, which he passed along to my sister Bonny.

When Bonny first spoke with the hospital staff, they alluded to a disagreement between the chief neurological surgeon and the younger neurosurgeon on call. Initially, they may have had different ideas about the appropriate action to take. Perhaps the seasoned surgeon thought it best to let Stacey stop breathing and die, given the massive head injury. We would come to know with certainty the younger surgeon's optimism and his indomitable resolution to save Stacey's life.

Troubled, I wondered if operating *might* save her life, why *not* operate? Why deliberate? Moreover, how would the decision to operate create a chain of events God could one day use for His glory?

Several years later, I asked the younger surgeon, Dr. Keith Kline, about the decision to operate, and he recalled:

It's possible the chief neurosurgeon may have suggested we let her go, and I said, 'No. We are going to operate.' If that was the conversation, then perhaps it did occur. I do not recall. But usually there's one attending on the case, and he's in charge.

The others are backups. He was my superior, but I was the one on the case.

My approach is always to assume the patients are salvageable, unless they come in and it's obvious—they have no heartbeat or something like that. We usually pull out all stops. I would doubt we would talk about that unless she was braindead on arrival, which you can't really determine initially. It's usually not the policy to discuss whether or not we should do something. We do everything possible to preserve life, especially with a young person. I was on call that day, the attending physician. I called the shots.

Nevertheless, it became obvious as the medical specialists made up their minds for the appropriate path to pursue, each remained convinced of his knowledgeable position. The younger doctor operated, beginning his fight to preserve her life and to maintain as much function as possible. The staff joined the battle and worked feverishly to keep her alive.

Ultimately, the decision to operate started a ripple, which gained momentum and tested my faith as never before. When I finally allowed the One who controls the ebb and flow of the earth's turbulent waters to control my own life, I discovered the stronghold of His enduring love, the powerful love that held my life together amidst this world's turmoil. Not until years later did I see how God had orchestrated every moment of that day, and how this ripple affected all of those who were close to Stacey. God had her days counted out. He had come into Stacey's life and mine *"for such a time as this."*

Coping Strategies

- Journaling: Keep a journal to record information and experiences. Write down your feelings, helpful comments from others, questions for the medical staff and their answers, meaningful Scriptures, and resources for future follow-up.

- Communication: Ask a close family member or trusted friend to facilitate communication via phone calls and emails, share updates, and coordinate everyday help. This will allow you to conserve your time and energy, and free you to respond to the issues that demand your attention. CaringBridge* offers free, personalized websites for sharing information.

- Guest book: A guest book in the hospital room allows visitors to make known their visitation, prayers, and thoughts.

*A list of resource information appears on page 211.

CHAPTER 4

Will She Live if You Don't Operate?

His words incised my heart.

M y sister Bonny worked the morning of the accident and arrived home around noon. Her memory of what happened next recounts an essential part of the story:

"I heard the phone ringing when I came in the door. Pappy sounded confused. Hobson Medical Center had called his house. Someone needed to go to the hospital because Stacey and her boyfriend had been in an accident. The hospital tried phone numbers of those who lived nearby with the same last name of Magargle until they reached someone who knew Stacey. They finally reached Pappy Magargle.

"'Can you go to the hospital? Pappy asked. 'I don't feel well enough, and I need to stay here and take care of Grammy.' Pappy had just been diagnosed with cancer. From the anxiety in his voice, I knew he couldn't have handled the trip to Hobson. I assured him I would go.

"I called the hospital and reached the social worker with whom Pappy had spoken. They still hadn't reached Nancy and Ronnie. The social worker said they needed someone from the family to come to the hospital as soon as possible. They already had Marcus in surgery and were trying to keep Stacey alive, trying to stabilize her until they could reach someone from the family. The social worker said Stacey had a severe brain injury.

"Her skull had been cracked open in the accident and the doctors were trying to decide whether or not to operate. They needed direction from the family. They said she was not yet stable, and they couldn't operate until they could get her vital signs under control. But once they stabilized her, they needed to have permission from the family to operate.

"'Will she live if you don't operate?'" I asked.

"'Probably not,'" the social worker told me.

"'Of course you can operate. Do everything you possibly can for Stacey!' I hung up the phone and threw it on the table, furious they would even consider not operating.

"Around 3:30 p.m., I arrived at Hobson. The hospital chaplain and the social worker took me upstairs where I found Heather and her mother.

"The chaplain told me Stacey was still in surgery. I waited—and waited. Why Stacey with all her potential? I couldn't believe it.

"Finally, Dr. Kline left the surgical ward and met with me in a conference room.

"'She made it through the surgery. She's stable. We won't know more until she regains consciousness. We removed a portion of the right frontal lobe of her brain.'

"He made it sound like it wasn't such a big deal because they had only taken as much as needed where bone fragments had lodged in the tissue. He said the left side didn't appear to have sustained as much damage. In retrospect, I understand everything was tentative. Only time would tell the extent of Stacey's brain injury.

"The neurosurgeon said he had removed the contaminated tissue and shattered fragments. He explained the injury. He told us the incredible force of the impact had exposed a section of her brain. He compared her broken skull to a crack in an eggshell. Because of this break, she had survived. It alleviated some of the inner cranial pressure. Otherwise, she probably would not have lived long enough to undergo the surgery.

"I thought the remaining portion of the brain controlled speech and music. When I first told others about Stacey's injury, I mistakenly told them she would still be able to both talk and sing because her injury involved the right side of the brain. Unfortunately, I misunderstood. Stacey might have regained ability to speak, but she would never sing again. "Only the future would tell how gravely mistaken I was.

Music in the Mind

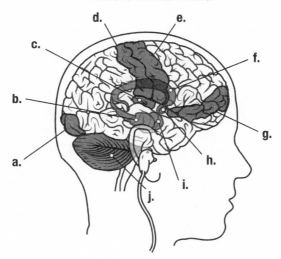

a. **Visual Cortex**
Reading music, looking at a performer's or one's own movements.

b. **Hippocampus**
Memory for music, musical experiences and contexts.

c. **Auditory Cortex**
The first stages of listening to sounds. The perception and analysis of tones.

d. **Sensory Cortex**
Tactile feedback from playing an instrument and dancing.

e. **Motor Cortex**
Movement, foot, tapping, dancing, and playing an instrument.

f. **Corpus Callosum**
Connects left and right hemispheres

g. **Prefrontal Cortex**
Creation of expectations, violation and satisfaction of expectations.

h. **Nucleus Accumbens**
Emotional reactions to music.

i. **Amygdala**
Emotional reactions to music.

j. **Cerebellum**
Movement such as foot tapping, dancing, and playing an instrument. Also involved in emotional reactions to music.

Bonny continued:

"During our first meeting with Dr. Kline, I asked about Marcus. The social worker had told me the only other person involved was the young man driving the car. The doctor said he was stable. His family sat in the same waiting room as we did. Heather told me who they were. I didn't speak with them until they asked me if Stacey had made it through the surgery.

"I never saw his family again, although I did go in to see Marcus. His nearly naked body, stitched together in lines running from the bottom of his legs, up his torso, across his chest, and down the length of his arms, glistened from sweat. Nurses told me he had a high fever.

"At the sight of Marcus, my mind darted back to Stacey. Denial and shock seized me. I thought Stacey would be like Joni Eareckson Tada, a paraplegic author, painter, and singer, who had risen above her physical handicaps and had begun a powerful worldwide ministry. Perhaps Stacey would be paralyzed, but she'd still be able to communicate, still our same Stacey. But when I went in to see her, I couldn't possibly recognize her.

"I couldn't believe what I saw. I tried to find a strand of her hair to see if it felt like hers. All you could see were her closed eyes, nose, and mouth. But they were all grossly swollen, so the person lying before me did not even resemble our beautiful Stacey.

"The social worker and chaplain both reassured and encouraged me, 'Go ahead … talk to Stacey, take her hand, and hold it in yours.' I saw the little mole on her wrist. This really *was* our Stacey.

"'It's Aunt Bon, Stace. You're going to be all right.'

"I stayed and talked to her as long as I could and kept checking with the social worker to see how soon her parents might arrive. Sometime in the afternoon, my sister Mary Ann and her family came. Others didn't get to the hospital until evening. All throughout the afternoon and evening, Mary Ann kept asking the floor nurse if there was any new information on Stacey's condition."

———

When I interviewed Dr. Kline in 2009, he shed more light on the first critical decision to operate:

"When we couldn't reach you or her father for permission to operate on Stacey, the social worker asked your sister Bonny for permission.

"Bonny asked, 'Will she live if you don't operate?'

"The social worker said, 'Probably not.' That was correct.

"When your sister said, 'Yes, operate.' Boom! Then you start this whole cascade because that's a major point at initial treatment. Are you 100 percent go for the goal? We need to rely on the family to tell us what the patient would want. Stacey couldn't tell us anything."

———

Later that evening, long after the surgery, Ronnie and I arrived at the hospital.

I didn't hear what took place during those first critical hours until after we saw Stacey for the first time. Walking into the emergency room entrance felt like walking into another world. I looked into the faces of all Stacey's loved ones. The thought of losing her nearly knocked me over. Fear and dread flooded over me. I felt as if a thousand hours had passed since the time we first heard of Stacey's accident. Until now, adrenalin had propelled my thoughts and prayers. Weakness and trepidation now ambushed me.

The operation had taken place hours earlier. The physician had already left the trauma unit, so we had to reach him by phone.

Our family stood, gathered around my husband and me, as the chaplain tenderly sat us down to make the call. Ronnie held the phone first but soon looked as if he might faint and go into shock. I took the phone from him, cradled it in my hand, and huddled closer to Ronnie, so we both could hear what the doctor said. I think I repeated most of what I heard. I, too, must have gone into some kind of shock as the doctor described Stacey's injury.

"… Severe open-head trauma[6] with a large defect on the right side. … I removed part of Stacey's brain."

Dr. Kline performed a procedure called a craniectomy[7] to help with intracranial hypertension. In this procedure, he removed a portion of Stacey's skull on the right side to allow her brain to swell without being confined within the cranium. He mentioned something about a problem with intracranial pressure—the difficulty they had maintaining normal pressure within her skull even after removing a section of it.

His words sounded like a foreign language. I wanted to stop him, to ask, "Is it my daughter you are talking about? Could this be happening to my Stacey? Are you sure we are talking about the same person?"

Of course, he couldn't hear my questions. They went unspoken. What would I know to ask? I knew nothing of such injuries. Nevertheless, he continued, oblivious to my inability to process what he said.

Stacey's head had slammed against the car. Her brain lacerated—gashed open from the impact.

He spoke of another complication: DIC (disseminated intravascular coagulation). When the brain sustains such an injury, the whole body releases anticoagulation substances to prevent clotting. This is a critical problem because once it starts, the entire body's affected and can sanguinate as the body bleeds to death internally.

Stacey could lose all her blood as each organ struggles to deal with and compensate for the crisis. "Stacey has a 40 percent chance of making it. She could die tonight."

I blanked out much of what I thought or felt. His description of our child's injury, her brain torn open, stunned me. He used the medical terminology of his trade—precise, razor-sharp words—to explain and assess our little girl's fragile condition.

His words incised my heart just as deeply as his scalpel had penetrated my daughter's skull to cut away portions of her brain. Only now, the surgeon's incision cut even deeper into me. His acerbic words stabbed me. My heart bled. He wounded the innermost part of my being. Did he mean to tear open my soul? The phone dropped from my hand.

I'm told others cried. Not me. I didn't cry. An icy sensation ran through my veins and penetrated deep into my bones. Newfound strength coursed through me. My whole body trembled. Ronnie took the phone and listened as the doctor finished his assessment, concluding with a few hopeful words regarding her recovery. The doctor spoke with dogged optimism—determined Stacey would survive.

Bewildered, I stood and softly pleaded, "Take me to her." The hospital corridor eerily morphed into a house of horrors. The walls cast distorted shadows, enshrouding me. The floor seemed to rise up beneath me with each step. Waves of nausea threatened; I fought back. The nurse led Ronnie and me to Stacey's bedside. It all felt surreal.

Upon seeing our daughter for the first time after the surgery, Ronnie became ill. He frantically left her bedside and ran to find the nearest restroom. Concerned, my brother Drexel followed him. Ronnie's stomach lurched until everything inside emptied into the toilet. This feeling of hollow emptiness continued with both of us for months and years.

When I first saw Stacey, even throughout this ordeal, I didn't acknowledge the layers of head wrappings or grotesque swelling. Others did. Her misshapen appearance simply did not register. She was our daughter. To me, she looked like my Stacey, but with a bandage covering her silky brown hair, or what remained of it. I only saw how much she needed me to take care of her. But how?

Strange thoughts enter a mother's mind when her child is broken. *Oh Stace, you just got a perm last week so you'd be all fixed up to leave for college. Look at this mess. Poor baby. We need to do something about it.* Nurses wrapped and rewrapped the head dressing. Within days of the accident, every curl straightened. What the surgeon hadn't shaved away grew dull and lifeless.

The first night, we all gathered around her bed and talked to Stacey. The medical staff told us to do and say things to try to initiate some response from her. My seven brothers and sisters can be rowdy. We did crazy antics to try to illicit some reaction from Stacey, desperate for even the slightest response. We laughed—that kind of crazy-nervous laugh that makes no sense. We recited a nonsense poem my brother-in-law had taught the little ones earlier in the summer.

"Oooey gooey was a worm, a mighty worm was he. ... "

We prayed and sang hymns and other songs. "Stacey loves *Les Miserables*. Maybe we could wake her with a show tune." We belted out, "Master of the house, doling out the charm ... "

"How about an oldies tune or one from church camp? Surely she'll respond to music." Oh, how I wish she had. But she didn't—not the first night or anytime thereafter.

My brother-in-law, Pastor John, later told me, "Unsure of her relationship with God, the spiritual condition of her heart, I asked God to give me the opportunity to pray with her. Sometime within the first forty-eight hours, Wally and Steven (my brothers) stood with me beside her bed. Steven read the Bible to her. I prayed the sinner's prayer and asked, 'Do you understand me, Stace? Is your heart right with God? Grip my hand if you understand and if you have your heart right with God.' She squeezed my hand. I felt her squeeze my hand—an indication she and God were okay."

Doctors later told us, " ... given the magnitude of her injury and extremely invasive surgery, Stacey could not have been minimally conscious even on the first night." Nevertheless, only the Lord knows if she had any meaningful response during John's prayer. However, weeks later, our merciful Heavenly Father would assure me of her secured relationship with Him.

Stacey's Uncle John went with her cousin Andrew to the police barracks to retrieve her personal effects. There they saw Marcus's car, what Ronnie later described as "a piece of %$@* Cavalier." John told us, "The passenger's side's crushed in from top to bottom. Somebody at the police barracks told us the paramedics found Stacey crumpled in a ball underneath the glove compartment."

John and Andrew brought back the Pennsylvania State Police evidence. John handed me the manila envelope. Before I looked inside, I read what was handwritten on the front: the identification data, the incident number, the property log number, and the signature of the investigating officer. A list of the contents followed: "one brown wallet with a various assortment of cards and $37.00 in US currency."

"This is it?" *How impersonal,* I thought.

I never saw the official police report. Because the court considered Marcus a juvenile, the case report would be sealed for his protection. I knew enough. Stacey lay critically injured. I didn't need the report. I did need to figure out how to take care of our daughter.

In the following days, I looked at the contents of the envelope and handled them repeatedly along with some of her other stuff: her glasses, her pink overnight bag, her shoes, and so on. One small bag held the meager remnants of that awful day. I wept as I ran my hand over her leather purse. *Why had she thought it necessary to work when she could have come with us? She shouldn't be lying here so broken.* I handled the pink bag as though its contents might disintegrate. How many times had I seen her pack it? Would she ever again enjoy sleepovers with her girlfriends? I slipped her high-school ring on my finger and didn't remove the gold band for months.

Later I tried to capture her fragrance, some scent of her still lingering in her bedroom. I hugged her stuffed animals and bathed them in my tears. I hungered for her touch, even to touch the things she had touched—for anything to make me feel closer to her, to make her more alive to me.

I doubt any of us slept the first twenty-four hours. Ronnie and I spent the first night with Stacey in her room. I tossed and turned on one of the chairs beside her bed while Ronnie spent all night at her side, alert. The pressure in her brain spiked during the long, silent hours. When morning dawned, he told me to prepare myself for the worst.

Bonny's question and her immediate response set us on a course, eventually involving three hospitals, countless medical professionals, meticulous and exhaustive neurological and physical exams, extremely invasive procedures for Stacey—and excruciating decisions for us.

I would have asked the same question Bonny asked: "Will she live if you don't operate?"

I would have screamed the same answer. "Yes. Yes. Yes. Operate. Please. Operate. Save her life!"

Having chosen this path, we would need God's wisdom and direction as never before.

Coping Strategies

- Make it easy on yourself: Take advantage of facilities, such as House of Hope and Ronald McDonald House, where you can eat and rest while remaining in close proximity to your loved one. These charities serve children and families around the world through family-centered programs, which promote health, healing, and togetherness. Stephen Ministries is another resource that provides caring support.

- Laugh: Like a release valve on an overfilled tire, laughter can bring relief.

CHAPTER 5

The Nightmare
Was Real

*The LORD is near to the brokenhearted
and saves those who are crushed in spirit.*

(Psalm 34:18)

Minutes melted into hours, hours into days. Some of our family and friends who wanted to remain close spent the nights with relatives who lived nearby. After Ronnie and I spent three or four sleepless nights at her bedside, someone arranged for us to stay at the Hobson Heritage house, a facility for the families of terminally-ill hospital patients.

We both collapsed unto the bed and retreated into the safety of each other's embrace. Ronnie drew me close and said, "You need to prepare yourself for the worst."

Somehow, his words drew me even closer to him. Never before had I felt this close to Ronnie. Intimacy enveloped us as we lay in each other's arms. Only the common bond shared by watching our child struggle to live surpassed the physical intimacy that brought her into the world.

Or was Stacey struggling to die? Had she begun a dying process over which God alone stood sovereign?

Stacey will be okay tonight, I reasoned. *She'll be in His hands. After all, He is the Lord of Life. He holds her in His all-powerful arms.* I felt a remarkable assurance. He had inclined His ear to hear our prayers. We had His full attention.

Exhausted, we drifted off to sleep.

Too early the next morning, I jolted awake. *What if I just don't open my eyes? Am I dreaming? Did the accident really happen? Was the doctor really talking about our daughter?*

But I couldn't wake from the nightmare. I couldn't escape the biting memory. I opened my eyes and began to walk into the longest, darkest months of my life.

I don't remember bathing, dressing, or eating breakfast. I needed to be with Stacey. We arrived at the hospital and met Dr. Kline at Stacey's bedside in the trauma ward. Since I had slept some the night before, I could now absorb more of the details he shared about Stacey's surgery, her condition, and prognosis.

Stacey remained critically ill. We had seen no change in her over the past three days, no sign of her opening her eyes and no sign of her coming back to us. Little had changed in her physical appearance or medical evaluation. Every time the doctor repeated what the medical tests revealed, the information sank in a bit deeper. She would have died if she had sustained a *closed*-head injury. The brain would have herniated down. She would have stopped breathing. She would have been clinically brain-dead.

However, Stacey had sustained an *open-skull fracture*[8] and a brain laceration with a great deal of swelling. He explained that when the brain incurs a cut, bleeding presents a critical problem because the ability to clot is severely compromised. Spontaneously, everything else in the body starts to bleed as it works to dissolve the clots quickly. Stacey didn't bleed to death because they surgically removed the damaged tissue and then immediately infused blood products to help reverse this natural response. The procedure had prevented her from bleeding out and had helped stabilize her. Even so, Stacey had already developed hematomas (clots) in the brain and was in a coma, each a major concern.

A ventilator with a tube in Stacey's mouth going into her lungs breathed for her. If she did well, they would remove the tube. If she couldn't breathe well on her own, they would reinsert it. They chose not to do a tracheotomy[9] because she breathed with the support of the ventilator.

In lieu of a direct IV line, a second tube fed from Stacey's mouth into her intestinal tract through which she received nutrition. Vedadines (devices attached to her legs) intermittently squeezed to prevent clots.

Dr. Kline had surgically removed the necrotic tissue composed of dead brain cells and debris from other dying cells. He eliminated the exposed, contaminated dead areas, which included the right anterior half of the temporal lobe, approximately the diameter of a fifty-cent piece.

I had no idea if that amount of brain tissue represented a large or small quantity. What did it mean for Stacey?

Dr. Kline continued with more details of what had happened and what we might expect. He discussed the possibility of bacterial pneumonia for which they would administer antibiotics. The brain laceration, damage because of severe edema (interstitial fluid causing swelling in the tissue), and hemorrhages disrupted or destroyed many of the pathways her brain formerly used. "To maximize Stacey's potential for recovery, occupational and physical therapists will try to stimulate brain activity, which will hopefully create new pathways to the same function."

"Hopefully" was the key word to which I cleaved. Glancing at Stacey's broken body, my tear-filled eyes brimmed.

Dr. Kline said brainstem evoked stimulations would identify the kind of activity in her brain. Evoked potential tests[10] would measure electrical activity in certain areas of the brain in response to visual, auditory, and sensory input. He planned to place wires on Stacey's scalp over areas on the brain to record the effects of stimulation on various parts of her body.

The swelling (edema) and intracranial pressure appeared to be Stacey's most urgent complications. Dr. Kline said, "We've done all we can to minimize the brain swelling. The cranial pressure is still not stable. It could escalate again, causing more damage or even her death."

Incredible! Even though they removed part of Stacey's skull, the critical problem of intracranial pressure continued. Until the swelling went down, they could not determine the amount of brain tissue destroyed or the remaining amount of healthy tissue.

I envisioned my precious daughter hooked up to electrical wires like Frankenstein's monster, a hole in her skull, and part of her brain now gone forever. "Oh Stace, I'm so sorry. I wish I could change all of this." My heart ached to be able to undo the damage, to rewind this reel as one rewinds a tape recorder to erase mistakes.

Dr. Kline said, "Although, we removed a large portion of Stacey's brain, I believe what tissue remains can learn new neural pathways. Your daughter could one day leave this hospital with some degree of function. How much function? We don't know."

He explained each side of the brain, or hemisphere, is dominant for specific behaviors although they are connected; they work together and share information. She would most likely regain her ability to speak because the left side of the brain, not as intrinsically affected by the trauma, dominates this function. Because the left side also dominates for calculations, math, and logical abilities, the doctor's prognosis favored Stacey regaining some of those abilities. However, because the right side is dominant for spatial abilities, facial recognition, visual imagery, and music, we might never hear her sing again.

I whispered, "Oh, Stace, I would miss hearing you sing, watching you practice at the piano. He said you might not even recognize us. We might have lost part of you, but Baby Doll, did you hear what the doctor said? Not all is lost."

So, she'll never be the same Stacey. I see the swelling. My devotion to her drove me to see beyond it or to vault over it or maybe to plunge deeper, wide-eyed, searching. *I know she's in there—somewhere.* "We'll figure this out. We love you, no matter what."

The straightforward diagnosis stunned everyone, and the complicated and tenuous prognosis grieved us. Emphatically, Dr. Kline maintained, "Part of Stacey's brain is still alive. But there's still too much swelling to give an accurate evaluation or to identify the residual effect of the trauma. We can only wait to see the extent of the present injury and hope nothing more happens to further damage other parts of her brain."

When the doctor paused, I jumped at my chance to ask a question. "Have you ever had a patient with this type of injury where you had to actually remove part of the brain?"

"I've had a few cases with similar injuries."

I braced myself against Stacey's bedrail. "Their outcome?"

"Well, one case involved a gunshot wound to the head, biparietal. I went ahead and debrided the injury and operated. The patient spent weeks and weeks in intensive care and physical therapy. Six months later, he walked into my office. He did have a limp, and he couldn't yet speak as fluently as before—but he could talk, and he could walk. He had a lot of function left."

Dr. Kline looked at Stacey then back to us. "Don't give up. Stacey's not brain dead. We haven't lost her yet. Other than her brain injury, she's in perfect health. She can still make it."

I latched onto the doctor's optimism with a vice-like grip. The doctor's words echoed within me.

> God, You can take this terrible situation and turn it around for Your glory. Stacey's brain isn't dead. She may be severely, even critically, injured—but she's not dead, God. You must not be ready to take her to Heaven yet. Lord, please, we need You to do Your part. Please heal her.

I prayed. I hoped.

———

Family, friends, and clergy from churches across the country began to pray for Stacey. My mother, a great prayer warrior, enlisted an army of believers from national ministries to join us in the battle for Stacey's life and recovery.

To cover all the bases, in case my prayers were somehow not getting through—perhaps blocked by my own sin or selfish motives—I asked children's Sunday school classes to pray. The prayers of innocent children would certainly engage a response from our Heavenly Father. Surely, those of an innocent child would get His attention. Surely, he couldn't refuse *them*.

Over the next week, children sent in sweet pictures depicting their pleas to God. When the nurses moved Stacey to a private room, we hung those drawings all over the walls, even re-hanging them as the staff moved her from room to room, hospital to hospital. I'm convinced God heard every prayer raised by faith as His children called on the name of Jesus Christ to heal our daughter.

One day, my mother, sister, and I took a break while medical personnel performed tests. Buried in the maze of hospital corridors, we found the chapel, a tiny, unadorned room. Opening the door, I glimpsed at the meager furnishings: a simple kneeling bench with a religious picture hanging over it, modestly situated at one end of the room while straight-backed chairs lined the other walls.

We saw one other person, a young woman, seated just inside the chapel door. Everything about her, her plain clothing, her long straight hair, her ordinary face, unembellished, made her the type of person who would not necessarily stand out in a crowd. She possessed serenity and beauty—elusive beauty if one looked only on the surface. Nevertheless, something struck me about this young woman.

Although I don't remember much of our conversation, I have a vivid memory of asking her, "Are you an angel?" I can't explain what prompted my unabashed question apart from her serene countenance. Was she meditating?

Compassion flowed from her, and peace appeared to envelope her and spread throughout the room like a fragrant aroma. Her eyes emanated pathos and empathy, imparting an aura of healing peace. An angel? Sent from God? I wonder now, if not an angel, perhaps Jesus Christ Himself sat with us and shared in our sorrows.

Whatever the case, we felt Jesus' presence there in one form or another. I am sure. I felt His love. I knew He cared about what we were going through. I knew He understood the gravity of the situation and shared in our anguish and grief. I cried out to God and took heart in knowing "the LORD is near to the brokenhearted and saves those who are crushed in spirit. ... The LORD redeems the soul of His servants, and none of those who take refuge in Him will be condemned" (Psalm 34:18, 22).

God had allowed Stacey to be grievously injured; yet, I believed He continued to keep guard over her. He would not allow her to die until He completed the plan He had for her life. He had already done the work of redeeming her soul when she accepted Him as her Lord, entrusting her life to Him. Her body, soul, and spirit belonged to Him. At that moment, I started to relinquish my control, asking for His will to be done in our daughter's life. It wasn't the first time nor the last I would give up and ask God to take over.

Meanwhile, doctors, interns, nurses, physical therapists, occupational therapists, respiratory therapists and on and on streamed through her room. I witnessed an inspiring commitment of the medical staff's sacred oath to do everything possible to promote recovery. Their devotion awed me. They each worked to ensure a good outcome for our daughter.

Sometime during the first week, an entourage of young interns paraded through the trauma ward behind the hospital's head neurosurgeon. Beds lined the walls. Cloth curtains separated one critically injured person from another. The ward reminded me of a scene from an old movie, an army medical ward perhaps, only more sterile.

I stood behind a column, peeking around the corner, concealed from their view, yet within earshot. Did this doctor have any more information, maybe a different approach, a new technique for treatment—something in which to place our hope? I prayed it would be so. The prestigious doctor lifted Stacey's chart from the foot of the bed, glanced at it disinterestedly, and then methodically placed it back in its holder.

"This one should be dead."

Not missing a beat, he abruptly walked on to the next patient. No further comment. And, it appeared, with no further thought of my daughter. He moved on to his next case.

What! What do you mean? Nothing more to say? I shriveled deeper into the crevice of the wall. *At the very least, couldn't your interns learn something from our daughter—even if you do think "this one should be dead"?* My fury never found its voice.

I don't know why I didn't confront him. Why I didn't run over, furiously shake him, and shout at the top of my lungs, "That's my daughter lying there. Pay some attention to her. Regardless of your opinion, she's not dead! Take care of her. For God's sake, it's your job!"

But I didn't. I never confronted him. Not then, not ever. Shocked, I didn't want to think what he said could even be remotely true. Maybe I didn't know what to say or think. The very idea of simply letting her die without trying to save her life appalled me. The thought sickened my heart, alien to my instinct. The doctor's abrupt, matter-of-fact attitude and dismissive words slammed me in the gut.

No other person at Hobson displayed such an attitude. Nevertheless, the sting of his cold pragmatism would assail me in the future.

Unconvinced and unsure of God's plan for Stacey, I refused to give up and let her die. God would teach me much more about the sovereignty of His plans in the weeks and months to come.

However, for the time being, this nightmare was all too real.

Coping Strategies

- Ask: If you don't understand something, ask questions. Find out what time the doctors make rounds and, if possible, prepare your questions before they arrive.

CHAPTER 6

The Illusion of Control Becomes the Idol of Control

Many plans are in a man's heart,
but the counsel of the LORD will stand.

(Proverbs 19:21)

I felt helpless and lost. This experience drove me to my knees, to the Savior whom I came to know as a child.

Nature draws me. I have vivid memories of one particular scene when, as a young girl, I stood on Vesper Hill at summer camp. The beautiful rolling mountains of Pennsylvania surrounded me:

A stream runs through the lush woodlands of the campground, gently tumbling over moss-covered boulders. I stand upon a carpet of spongy pale green lichens. The air is thick, balmy. My skin is damp with the dew of dusk. Nightingales flit overhead. They sweetly welcome the twilight and greet each other while crickets and peepers wake up to join the chorus of the brook's meandering melody. I gaze into a canopy of iridescent stars. Their brilliance illuminates a canvas of deep, velvety, jet-black sky.

Surrounded by the perfection of nature, awed by the excellence of God as displayed in His creation, my imperfection stands in stark contrast. In comparison to the immensity of God's creation, the majesty of His power portrayed within it, I feel small, insignificant.

I ask God, "Will you be part of my life? Can I be part of Yours?"

He responds to my heart's yearning, "Come, little one; take my hand. I'll show you the way."

That night, I put my trust in the One who held those stars in the sky and asked Him to hold *my life* in His hands.

Now I asked God to hold *our daughter's life* in His hands.

Still, in the days and weeks to come, I would struggle to release Stacey to Him. My inability to completely trust God revealed a destructive attitude of control in me. Without realizing it, over the years, I gradually exchanged the security of my relationship with Christ for the false security of my own imperfect knowledge and limited ability to work things out for myself. I firmly believed in God at the time of our daughter's accident, but this crisis shook the foundations of that faith.

On the surface, we looked like the all-American family. By this time, Ronnie and I had been married twenty-three years. My husband had a great job as chief executive officer over a successful manufacturing company. Our kids, bright, healthy, and full of energy, played sports, took music lessons, and generally kept us busy.

Throughout our marriage, my husband's work and hobbies left me alone with the kids much of the time. When faced with the void in my relationship with Ronnie, I buried myself in the responsibilities of home, children, service organizations, and church. I felt painfully alone in rearing the children and caring for our home. This loneliness bred resentment. I grew bitter and angry, desperate for my husband's attention and approval.

I hid in relationships. I ran from confrontation. I feared letting others down: my co-workers, my friends, my children, and yes, even my husband. Above all, I feared I would let the Lord down. Desperation fueled my fears.

I struggled to make decisions. *What if I made the wrong choice? What if I displeased God with my decision?* Fear evolved into my need to control and trapped me in a vicious cycle. Looking back, I realize all my fears originated in, and were perpetuated by, one underlying cause: I lived unconvinced of God's enduring, unconditional love for me.

Fear threw me off balance when I thought I might miss God's direction regarding Stacey's care. I believed it was absolutely necessary to align with God's plan for Stacey and for me.

At the outset of Stacey's accident, my entire focus converged into three probing questions:

To the doctors: "What can *you* do for her?

To myself: "What can *I* do for her?"

To God: "What is *Your* will for Stacey?"

Those questions echoed in all my others and spawned my yearning for more information. "Please help me understand Stacey's injury." "Are you doing everything you possibly can for her?" "Can I help swab her mouth? Turn her over?"

Lord, I need to make sense of things, figure out Your plan for Stacey. And my part in it. Please help.

The medical jargon and its ramifications were beyond me. Maddening. Everything normal or routine disappeared. Control? Illusory. Had the earth's axis tilted slightly and thrown the world—my world—out of kilter?

Throughout the ordeal, each day unfolded with its own set of hurdles to overcome. With each new development, I questioned the physicians:

"How can we take care of this problem?"

"What do we face today?"

"What do we need to look for in this set of tests?"

There were endless inquiries, unrelenting and exhausting.

The medical staff responded to my need to understand Stacey's ever-changing condition with patience and respect. They answered the questions they could then tenderly said, "We need to wait and see."

My daily mantra became, "I just need a plan so I can handle these tests and to come to terms with their results. Then I'll deal with the next crisis."

If I knew what we faced on a certain day regarding her care and the status of her condition, which sometimes changed from moment to moment, I thought I could maintain some sense of control in this chaos. Otherwise, I might fall apart.

I stubbornly held onto this illusion of control.

Daily I pleaded with God: *Father, please give me the strength to handle what you allow in these next few moments. Then we'll move on together from here. I just need a plan to handle this one thing.*

I strained. I wrestled. I rarely rested.

Father, You have the power over life and death. The medical team doesn't. Help me to submit to You. Help me to rest in my prayer for Your will—not mine—to be done. Help me abide in the freedom of Your perfect love, not the fallacy of my perfection. Help me accept Your ways, even though I may never understand them.

God's promises of peace and strength carried me through the first days. However, they became harder to hold onto when the experience challenged my deepest spiritual beliefs and depleted my physical resources. It took me years to realize God had a plan—just one. I needed only to trust Him.

———

A few days after Stacey's accident, Dr. Kline informed us of an alarming escalation in Stacey's intracranial pressure. The conversation took place just outside Stacey's room. She still lay in the trauma unit, surrounded by other critically ill patients. We stood in the hall where there were no chairs, no privacy.

In spite of the removal of the brain flap, her brain continued to swell and squeeze through her skull. Dr. Kline's description of the fracture reminded me of a topographical map: "It's a markedly depressed comminuted skull fracture on the right frontal temporal region extending to the right petrosal ridge. In other words, the whole right side of her skull has cracks going through it.

"Think of it this way: if you take a ping-pong ball and push in, you get an indentation. Since Stacey's skull's not pliable like a ping-pong ball, the indentation looks like a satellite with star-shaped cracks radiating all the way over the top and base of the skull, covering 80 percent of the right side of her skull. Stacey's brain continues to swell out of the opening, another indication of just how severe the fracture.[11]

"When we see these high levels of intracranial pressure, we wonder is it because of the cranial monitor[12] we implanted during surgery or because of the brain. The waveform may be dampened if the catheter tip has shifted and is pressing against the ventricular wall or because a blood clot or an air bubble is plugging the fiberoptic sensor and giving false readings. We aren't sure which possibility could account for this pressure spike."

In the hallway, the cold reality accosted us. *Why did he pick this place to tell us? Why do I feel like a phantom just kicked me behind the knees?*

He continued. "CT scans show effuse swelling with some small intrapracamal hemorrhages which indicates more blood vessel disruption. This extreme elevation in pressure poses a critical concern. Her brain may herniate down within the next few hours. If it does, she'll stop breathing and die or, at least, be clinically brain dead at that point."

My stomach churned. Terror tore at my throat. *Where can I run to escape these words?*

"We just don't know. It might just be the monitor has shifted. Only time will tell us what's happening."

Breathe. Lean hard into the wall. I tried to take it in. I really did try. *Oh, Lord, keep me standing. I need to hold it together.*

We had spent the first nights at the hospital then at the Hobson Heritage House. It was not home and not our bed. Our bodies knew it. I struggled to maintain some semblance of physical composure while my mind reeled under the weight of the possibility of Stacey's imminent death. I listened to the doctor's conclusion: "All we can do is wait."

All we can do is wait. Nothing but wait.
How will You handle this new crisis, Lord? How will I?
We waited. Helpless.

I prayed. Hopeful.

Over and over, like a stubborn child trying to wear out—or wear down—a parent, I pleaded:

Lord, if You are going to allow something this horrible to happen to Stacey, You must receive glory from it somehow, someday. God, You hold the stars in the sky, You control the whole universe. You must have a purpose. You promise to cause all things to work together for good to those who love You, to those who are called according to Your purpose (Romans 8:28). I'm holding You to Your promise. I love You, Lord. Stacey loves You. I want only Your will. No matter how this turns out, if Stacey lives or dies. I cannot bear this unless I know You will be glorified through it.

Had God allowed this injury to be so extensive, so critical in order to show Himself strong—stronger than medical science, stronger than procedures and prognosis? The situation careened completely out of our hands. Even now, the doctors admitted the futility of predicting an outcome either way.

Any moment she could die. I understood all too well. The reality stabbed at my heart, testing my deepest convictions and beliefs. Did I truly believe in eternal life? Did I believe Stacey would live in Heaven with God if she died tonight? I realized Stacey knew *about* God. In our home, I'd rejoice when I'd see her lying on her bed reading her Bible. Yes, she had her quiet times with God.

Yet, a vast difference exists between knowing *about* someone as opposed to truly knowing them. God created Stacey to have a personal relationship with Him. She went to church and Sunday school and attended church youth group events—associations and activities which prepare one for a spiritually centered life.

But, Lord, does she know you as her Savior? Does she believe You died to take the punishment for her sins? Who can work hard enough to get it all right, to understand Your ways, to always be in control of inner desires and motives, and to be perfect and never make a mistake? You say no one can (Romans 3:23).

I knew there were times when I rebelled against God. I knew Stacey wasn't perfect, either. We both needed a rescuer. I kept coming back to the truth I learned in my youth: The promise of eternal life rests solely in the work of Jesus. "Christ also suffered when he died for our sins once for all time. He never sinned, but He died for sinners that he might bring us safely home to God. He suffered physical death, but He was raised to life ..." (1 Peter 3:18, NLT).

Jesus Christ, God's only Son, provided the perfect sacrifice, His own life, for mankind and for Stacey. By His death, for all who believe, Jesus ensured fullness of life now and forever with God.

Is Stacey truly prepared to meet You if she dies tonight? Years ago, I saw her go forward in church. She then invited You into her life and asked You to forgive her sins. Her future now hinges on that decision.

God reminded me if Stacey died that night, I could count on Him to take care of her because "... to all who believe Him and accept Him, He gives the right to become children of God" (John 1:12, NLT).

I believed and firmly embraced these truths long before our daughter's accident. Yet, my beliefs had not come under the fire of testing—not until our dear Stacey lay in the hospital, lingering between life and death.

At the close of this harrowing day, I thanked the Lord for allowing my daughter to remain with me. Many more life-and-death developments threatened to take her from us during those first days at Hobson. The onslaught of each crisis sucked the breath from me. My only foothold was God's sovereignty. This certainty helped steady me as the ground shifted under my feet.

There were times when I feared I would collapse under the weight of each downward spiral. I sat beside our daughter. I waited for the next battery of tests to be done, waited for the next doctor's report, waited for God to answer our prayers to heal her, and waited for God to take her to be with Him. All the while, I waited for God to restore my peace of mind and heart. I found it harder and harder to rest in God. Tenuously, I clung to Him with all the strength I could muster.

In those dreaded angst-ridden hours, Jesus' voice came intermittently as faint whispers to my heart: "Take comfort, my child, I'm taking all Stacey's needs to our Father. All her desires. All her broken dreams. Yours, too."

Stacey's Your child, Lord. Your will be done. Each time I said those words I meant them. Yet, as one critical situation followed another, each carrying the possibility of her death, I unwittingly took her back from Him, resuming my relentless quest for medical information. I only understood a minuscule amount regarding Stacey's continued physical decline, and, even worse, my spiritual understanding became nearly as incomprehensible.

God knew I would need reassurance of our daughter's final resting place, and He continually assured me through the Scriptures and through the encouragement of pastors and friends. His peace and comfort quieted my mind and heart for a few blessed moments throughout each day. Nevertheless, I couldn't fully embrace these reassurances at the time. Other voices thundered in my ears and drowned out His voice: the doctors, their dismal reports, even my own voice: *Father, please help me be still so I can hear Your calm, sweet voice and follow You through this valley of the shadow of death. I won't stop trusting you.*

I clung to His promises as a frightened child clings to her mother's hand. He had prepared a way to rescue our daughter from death and me from any doubt, confusion, or regret. I needed to hear only one Voice, one Person, whose direction I needed to follow.

The Psalms reassured me God wanted to express His compassion—to comfort me, to cry with me. I wanted to walk in the freedom of His love, but the illusion of control had morphed into my golden cow. This idol stood as a barrier. Much more would happen before I released the "idol of control" and gradually surrendered to God's unconditional love.

He knew what would turn my mind and my heart from this idolatry. He knew exactly what it would take to adjust my mind to hear only His voice. I had not yet fully submitted to Him or listened to His voice above all others so I could be free to follow Him and free to respond to His love.

When will I hear your voice again, God? When will you restore my soul with Your peace? Will You heal Stacey's wounds? My wounds? Help me Holy Spirit to hear only my Father's voice. And help me to walk in His footsteps.

Our perfect God always stands by His word. If I relinquished my passion for control and turned to Him, then I would hear His voice above the distractions, above the clamor of medical tests, above my search for spiritual insight, and above my own screaming voice. Then I truly would be free (John 8:36).

At times, acutely aware of my passion for control, I would ask God to forgive me, trust Stacey's outcome to Him, and rest. Other times, I had no idea of the degree of inner turmoil taking place. Trying to understand something beyond my comprehension became the only way I could hold onto some illusion of control.

In reality, I had no control.

Stacey's life, as we had known it, little by little, slipped away.

Coping Strategies

- Professional resources: Utilize the support of the facility's chaplains, clergy, counselors, social workers, human resource department, and others.
- Admit your weakness to God. Depend on His strength.

CHAPTER 7

Stubborn Hope

I still hold out hope Stacey's brain is recovering.

Dr. Kline

Time marched on. A constant factor. Was it an enemy or a friend? Dr. Kline had said, "The first twenty-four hours are critical to Stacey's survival and outcome. If she lives that long, her chances for recovery improve."

Twenty-four hours later, we thought we could breathe easier. But one crisis followed on the heels of another.

"She could be gone within minutes."

A mother can hardly bear hearing those words even just one time. But again and again? The doctors repeatedly cautioned us to prepare for the worst. Did God hear? Did He listen? Did Stacey continue to suffer further damage?

Dr. Kline tried to explain:

The extensive swelling makes it difficult to identify the immediate damage and impossible to predict the extent of residual damage. When injured, the brain initially goes through stages of swelling.

This swelling doesn't peak until the third or fourth day after surgery and may last up to two weeks. The edema interrupts the insulating sheaths of the nerves. Initially, you get more dysfunction from swelling, but that's reversible. It can heal. It can improve over the next weeks and months as the nerves find new pathways and re-circuit."

It can heal. It was a lifeline to hold, a lifetime to hope.

If only we knew how long that life would last.

I believed God had created Stacey. I borrowed the Psalmist's words to pray for her:

You knitted [Stacey] together inside [me]. [Her] bones were not hidden from You when [she] was made in secret, when [she] was skillfully woven in an underground workshop. Your eyes saw [her] when [she] was only a fetus. Every day of [her] life was recorded in Your book before one of them had taken place. How precious are Your thoughts concerning [her] O Lord." (Psalm 139:13, 15–17, GWT)

From conception, He had made her. He held the power to create new brain tissue if He chose to. I waited for God to make His next move. Would He heal her or take her to Heaven? We would know in time, His time.

I looked to God. I watched over Stacey. I ached for more time with her.

I attended to her most rudimentary needs. To me, everything I did seemed insignificant. Still I welcomed the opportunity to do something—anything.

Stacey's hands contracted into vise-like fists, turning her knuckles white each time the ventilator mechanically forced air into her lungs. Her nails cut the palms of her hands as she clenched them. I thought, *if my words don't reach Stacey, if our prayers … well … maybe she can feel my hand on hers.* I pried open her hand. Damp fingers clamped around mine. I watched helplessly as Stacey moved spastically upon the bed.

"Baby Doll, remember when you were just a wee tyke, and we painted these nails?" *Does she even know I'm here?*

I trimmed her nails. Wrapped her palms in towels. "There now. Better."

I assisted nurses, gently repositioned her legs, arms, and torso. *Are there any bedsores? I can't see any. Thank God. Please, Lord, I want to keep her with us. Nevertheless, Your will be done.*

I ran the comb through her hair. "Oh Stace, it used to feel like corn silk. Where's the shine, the bounce?"

"Ugh!" I refused to submit. I shook off the melancholy and ran my hands through limp strands of lackluster hair. "Do you remember when you cut your doll's hair, Stace?" I chuckled. "I should say 'hacked.' You did the same to yours."

Dr. Kline said we'd know more in a few days. Maybe things will look better then. My chest heaved, and I let out a heavy sigh.

Day seven.

Dr. Kline's latest report threatened my hope for healing. "Stacey has not been minimally conscious, not even on the first night. She arrived in a coma. It hasn't changed. She still has no conscious awareness of her surroundings. Her brain's able to respond to certain things, but she has no conscious response, only reflexes."

The doctor may have talked forty-five minutes, but I remembered ten seconds, the time it took him to say, "[She] is able to respond."

I clutched what I thought I understood, what I heard as good news. Who wouldn't take it as a positive when the doctor initiated a response and Stacey reciprocated? Hope welled within me.

It was misdirected hope.

What I saw were "primitive responses to stimuli," inappropriate responses. Decerebrate posturing[13], as Stacey displayed, indicates massive brain injury extending to the brainstem. In reality, our daughter had so little undamaged brain tissue and so many damaged circuits that any messages went out as non-meaningful movements.

I comprehended very little at the time. I wrongly deducted, and tenaciously believed, those movements were a good sign. After all, day after day, Dr. Kline continued to be optimistic. I didn't yet grasp even a slight picture of the vast amount of damage Dr. Kline saw in his examination and neurological tests, despite his optimism.

Within days, another crisis occurred. The intracranial pressure monitor implanted at the time of surgery skyrocketed for the second time. Dr. Kline's report disheartened us:

Supposedly the monitor pressure will shift only a tenth of a millimeter a day, called "drift," so in a week it's only a few millimeters off. We're in our second week. Is Stacey's tissue still profusely swelling, or does the monitor sit in a blood clot? We can't tell for sure what's going on. The brainstem may hemorrhage at any time and go down. If this happens, she'll stop breathing and die within a very short time.

What? Not again. Stop! I wanted to cover my ears. *God, do You hear this? Should we still hope? Lord, why can't they figure out what's going on? They're the professionals. Why don't they know what's happening to Stacey?*

Hope dwindled. Pleading intensified. *Father, You alone know what's happening to our daughter. Please take care of Stacey. I trust You. You know best. If she stops breathing, I'll accept that as Your answer. If she continues to breathe, I will rejoice. Either way, I will praise You.*

Minutes, hours ticked by. I sat beside her, arrested by the terrifying possibility every breath could be her last. Hoping it wouldn't be.

Dr. Kline returned the next day with, yet, another dismal report:

Stacey continues to breathe, which indicates function in the lower brainstem. However, she does not spontaneously cough to clear her throat or lungs. She's developed bacterial pneumonia. Nevertheless, part of her brain is still alive at this point. She's not brain dead, and there's still hope. We just need to wait and see what happens. I still hold out hope Stacey's brain is recovering.

How long had I held my breath? Seconds? Minutes? My lungs burned. Would they collapse?

"We need to wait and see what happens?" I'll scream if I hear those words one more time. Will we ever see improvement? When will this torture end?

I wondered how Stacey felt. A chill crept over me as I stood gazing upon her sweat-glistened body, reaching for her hand, reaching for her. *What's this doing to you, Stacey, dangling between life and death? Are you in pain?*

The doctors said she felt no pain. *I* writhed in agony. Helpless to fix—anything.

God, where are You? Why don't You do something one way or the other? Do You hear me calling out? I can't hear You. Why don't I hear You?

When no answer came, I grilled the doctors and nurses for more information. The on-going search for God's will took a heavy toll. I watched over my sweet daughter, one minute praying, the next consumed with the urgency of her needs and the efficacy of her care. I didn't question God's power to heal her. I did question His intention.

"I'm here, Stacey. We're all here for you. So many have called to say they're praying for you. Can you hear your Uncle Steven reading David's Psalms?" *Do the Scriptures reassure her? Is her spirit even aware of our presence? She doesn't respond to anything.*

One of Stacey's cousins left CDs of Joni Eareckson Tada. "Drex Jr. brought a CD for you, Stace. I'll put it in when I leave this evening."

I hoped and prayed the inspirational recordings comforted Stacey. *But, Lord, does the music even reach her?*

Around day thirteen, Dr. Kline told us Stacey had suffered more hemorrhages, pressure spikes, convulsions, and various infections, which caused high fevers. "This damage has made it impossible for her to breathe effectively. More intracranial pressure spikes may have caused greater loss of viable brain tissue. There's still too much swelling to know for sure."

Only the fact she could still breathe registered in my brain. She still could move her hands and arms. She still had some degree of function.

In fact, Dr. Kline's voice rang in my ears with his resolute optimism. He held out hope the reflexes, though primitive, might indicate part of the midbrain had resumed function. "She closes and opens her eyes but there's no visual tracking yet. We see some movement in response to the ventilator and other stimuli. I still hold out hope Stacey's brain is recovering, and we will begin to see meaningful responses."

Dr. Kline threw me a lifeline of hope, a thin thread to clutch. I rejoiced to see Stacey's brain could still respond to certain things.

The first instant I saw Stacey open her eyes, I ran to get the nurse. "Look! She's waking up!"

As we rushed back to her room, I praised God. I thought maybe, just maybe, one day my little girl would walk out of there.

However, when I got back to her and looked into her eyes, all I saw were hollow, dull orbs. The life that once shone from them had disappeared. With it, a glimmer of my own life's light vanished.

The daily reports did not improve. Stacey continued to posture with no appropriate response to stimulation or verbal commands. The fevers worked against healing. The scans showed more bleeding.

Years later, the doctor clarified the details of Stacey's day-by-day decline:

We saw ... blood even appearing in the upper part of the brainstem. This usually indicates a rotational injury within the skull, but with so much swelling, we couldn't be sure. The two hemispheres of the brain come together at the brainstem. With a rotational injury, the point of twist occurs in the upper brainstem. The blood we saw in that area indicated there had been some shearing, probably from the force of the impact during the collision.

We could do nothing for the brainstem bleed because of its depth. We couldn't access the area even during surgery. Because of swelling, we still couldn't tell how much infarcted[14] brain tissue remained. It usually takes weeks, sometimes a month to tell.

By September 8, Dr. Kline's notes substantiated hydrocephalus.[15] There had been no improvement or stabilization of brain tissue although two weeks had passed. "Hydrocephalus," he said, "means Stacey's ventricles are swollen. The ventricles are pockets within the brain, which produce spinal fluid." Once again, his explanation sounded like a foreign language I desperately groped to comprehend.

Father, please help me concentrate. Please help me hear what he's saying. Help me understand what's happening to our daughter.

He put forth several reasons for the hydrocephalus—a lesson in physiology and anatomy I never signed up to take. He used such high and lofty language. With no escape from this living classroom of horror, I couldn't ignore the consequences for my daughter. I only knew I loved my little girl and wanted her to wake up, to come back to us. I hung on his every word, hoping for a morsel of good news. I remembered little. I understood less.

The rollercoaster of ups-and-downs and the sideswipe of blind corners threatened to spin me off track into oblivion. My physical, mental, and emotional resources dwindled. What did all this mean to our beloved Stacey? Her chances of survival, minimal when she arrived at Hobson, dwindled as well. She slipped farther away from us.

Dr. Kline continued to hold out hope. "Remember, we are going 100 percent for the goal."

I clung to the fragile thread of his unwavering optimism.

"I think she'll have some type of recovery. I'm still hoping she'll get well," Dr. Kline said. "I believe we can still win this one!"

Lord, He still believes this can turn around. I must believe. Please turn this around. You have the power. You promise all things work together for those who love You. I love You. Stacey loves You. Please heal my daughter.

Each day with no improvement lessoned the likelihood of significant recovery. Each crisis left in its wake devastation to her brain, destruction not immediately definable. Although we never pinpointed the precise moment, her brainstem did hemorrhage.

Stacey remained at Hobson for fifteen days. All the while, her brain swelling actually increased, and Stacey remained comatose;

this exacerbated the probability for improvement apart from a miracle. Looking back, Stacey seemed caught within the insidious tentacles of death. They silently crawled into her body, sucking the life out of her, destroying what healthy brain tissue remained.

It happened so stealthily. Unaware of the physical damage occurring within her, it took weeks and months, test after test after test, to convince me. We were slowly losing her.

Coping Strategies

- Research: Internet search engines can be helpful and informative, as long as one remembers to keep in mind the credibility of the source. Look for medical or scientific journals that have been published (online or print), as well as credible sites with ".org" or ".edu." For easy-to-understand definitions or explanations, Wikipedia is a good source, however, be aware that it may not contain the most comprehensive information.

CHAPTER 8

Who Really Cares About Stacey?

Our daughter's life is at stake.

I remained vigilant. Day after day, like a sentinel, I sat by her side as if Stacey's life depended upon my ability to protect her. Close proximity to her medical team assured me she received optimal care.

Ronnie and Rex returned to work after the first week. Summer vacation ended, and school started for Laura and Casey. They remained at home with Ronnie, three hours away from Stacey and me. With only a short break to go home and regroup, I returned to Hobson, joined by my oldest sister, Mary Ann.

In hindsight, I realize I probably understood so little about Stacey's condition at the time that my presence may not have made any difference. I could do little more than sit with her. Nevertheless, I ached to be close to our daughter. Being near her comforted me.

Twelve days after the accident, discussions started with Greyson Health Plan (GHP), our health-care provider. They wanted Stacey transferred to Greyson Medical Center (GMC) in Denton, fifteen miles from our home.

Nevertheless, Dr. Kline disagreed with GHP. He said she wasn't stable enough. Her nurses cautioned us not to even bump her bed because any jarring could harm her. They brought testing apparatus to her rather than move her to it. Now GHP wanted to load Stacey up and transport her to Denton. I panicked at the thought of moving Stacey before Dr. Kline approved the move. It didn't make sense.

The pressure to have Stacey moved to Denton intensified. A battle ensued between Hobson Medical Center and Greyson Health Plan. It came to a showdown between what Dr. Kline recommended and what GHP agreed to pay. GHP contended Stacey's condition had improved enough to transport to Denton. Furthermore, if she remained at Hobson, they'd refuse to cover the expenses.

Meanwhile, Dr. Kline remained entirely focused on his young patient.

Years later, I asked him about the situation.

"I don't remember the insurance issues," he said. "I had little interest in, or understanding of, the whole business part. I focused on the patient. Even now, years later, I want to have control because then I know everything is going well, especially when transporting someone. During transport, things can turn sour. But then you have the bean counters who 'know better.' I'm sure they looked at the two-week time course and said, 'She should be over her peak brain swelling; she can come to GMC now. It's safe.'"

At the time of Stacey's hospitalization, my own mode of operation had been simple. "I just need a plan, so I can handle the next few tests and digest their results." Shocked by that new dilemma, I never expected Stacey's medical care to be contingent upon insurance. I was so naive. I assumed Stacey's welfare elicited everyone's first priority. Did GHP truly care about our Stacey's recovery? Could I trust them, or were they mainly concerned about their financial bottom line?

We could not ignore that decision. We could in no way avoid the possibility of financial devastation. If GHP did not pick up the charges, we would be bankrupt. Nevertheless, foremost in my mind, lurked the potential threat the move held for Stacey. If we moved her now, could she recover?

Relentless, GHP continued to exert tremendous pressure to transfer her to Denton, while Dr. Kline held fast to his ground: "Stacey is not in any condition to transport."

How did we end up in a tug-of-war over my daughter's life? The Goliath on the other end of the rope posed a daunting threat to my daughter. How could Ronnie and I withstand them? How much more could we bear? It truly was infuriating. Why did money even factor into the equation?

Concerned about moving Stacey, Ronnie tracked down Dr. Kline and asked him pointedly, "How is she doing?" The doctor openly expressed his shock at the devastation he saw in the last exam to my husband.

Not until years later, did Ronnie finally tell me about that meeting with Dr. Kline shortly before Stacey's discharge from Hobson. I have no memory of either Dr. Kline or my husband sharing that harrowing news with me at that time. Why the doctor never conveyed to me his shock at the damage he saw even then, I don't know. Meanwhile, I grasped for the only way I knew to determine the truth.

Father, I feel like I'm losing it. Please give me the strength to handle what you allow in these next few moments. Please show me what's best for Stacey. I just need to know how to handle this one thing. Together we'll move on from here.

Who really cares about Stacey, Lord? Is our daughter some kind of pawn in a game? Well, I don't want to play. Our daughter's life is at stake! I don't know what to do … Should we allow her to be moved? Now?

That battle tore my attention from Stacey's care—what I wanted to be most important to everyone. Moving her threatened to impede her recovery and might even cause her death.

My husband and I felt cornered. Could they force us to make a decision? Hobson's staff had actively invested themselves and their resources on Stacey's behalf. They knew more about the care she needed than GHP. Yet, the insurance company threatened the very care Stacey required, the care we couldn't afford to provide if she remained at Hobson.

Like an angry polecat trying to protect its young, I vented to my sister and to my husband. "How dare they tell us to move her or they won't pay for her bills? Dr. Kline has had his hands inside Stacey's skull. I trust him. She's been traumatized enough without putting her through this before she's ready. If Dr. Kline doesn't think she's stable enough, she needs to stay put. That's *my* bottom line."

On the other hand, GHP had physicians and criteria of their own to determine the advisability of transfer. We were deadlocked while Stacey lay clenched in the ignoble vise of two monstrously large and powerful financial entities. GHP's threats continued.

My anxiety over this impasse neared the breaking point. My mind churned like a tightrope walker, slipping, teetering without my balancing pole. No longer able to concentrate solely on Stacey's care, my thoughts and emotions toppled. *Is this some kind of faith test? I'm not Job. Do I look like Job? I don't think I've got what it takes for this, Lord.*

Wrestling to figure this out, I remembered the story of Job. He struggled with his own uncertainties, but he didn't give up on God. Ultimately, he realized God's knowledge of all things eclipsed his own human ignorance.

But Job had a word from You, Lord. All these decisions. I want Your answer, Your direction.

Ironically, my sister-in-law, Sandy, worked as an insurance representative for GHP. Overwrought and disgusted, I called Sandy. "GHP and Hobson are fighting over her! Dr. Kline disagrees with GHP's assessment of Stacey. Can you find out anything? I don't know what to do."

Sandy recounted:

I immediately tried to reach the Vice President of GHP. We met in his office. I told him what was happening with GHP forcing this transfer. The VP told me GHP could *pressure* the family to transport the patient but could not *force* them to move her.

He felt Hobson simply didn't want to give up a patient for whom they were receiving dollar-for-dollar insurance reimbursement. He said GHP could not, in fact, demand her transfer. He led me to believe the attending physician was not acting in the family's best interest by refusing to release the patient to Greyson.

According to Greyson, the decision fell to Dr. Kline. Resistance from GHP to pay her bills if she remained at Hobson heightened each day while Dr. Kline insisted they were interested in finances, not in his patient. He wanted to keep Stacey where he could watch over her, to attend to her care personally. He insisted the problem was GHP. Yet, it appeared ultimately up to Dr. Kline to determine when Stacey could safely be transferred.

Shortly after my conversation with Sandy, she saw Dr. Imber, head of Greyson's trauma unit, and filled him in. According to her recollection, Dr. Imber responded bluntly, saying he didn't want to be part of it. He didn't say whether Stacey's condition warranted a move or not. He made it clear he did not want to discuss, or be involved with, the financial end of her care.

Years later, Sandy informed me, "Someone in the system had told me Stacey's care at Hobson neared the million-dollar figure. I'm sure Hobson profited each day Stacey remained their patient."

The financial statements we received later confirmed Stacey's care at Hobson had been a great expense but not nearly as high as Sandy had been told. Whether or not they significantly decreased day by day when she got to Greyson, I could not decipher from the bills. They appeared to me to be comparable. Nonetheless, because Hobson fell outside of GHP's plan, I became skeptical. I surmised finances accounted for a large part of the pressure to move her, and the sooner the better.

About this time, someone suggested I seek out the patient advocate for Hobson. After I spoke with her, the situation changed dramatically with lightning speed. The person who served as Stacey's advocate helped in ways of which I'm still uncertain. I know she talked with both Hobson and GHP. Within twenty-four hours, Dr. Kline okayed Stacey for transport. The uncertainty regarding which direction to take had been torture. With his approval, I felt at least a small degree of confidence Stacey could handle the transport. Ronnie remained uneasy with the situation.

Unfortunately, that part of the nightmare did not end there. More draining decisions lay ahead posed by another unexpected threat: the weather.

———◆———

My sister Mary Ann and I took care of the discharge arrangements at Hobson while Ronnie and Sandy waited for Stacey to arrive in Denton. Meanwhile, the command center at the Greyson Emergency Room communicated back and forth with the helicopter air-transport crew and Hobson.

Finally, the air-transport left Greyson and headed toward Hobson. However, electrical storms had begun to batter Hobson.

As the storms intensified, so did my fear over Stacey's precarious welfare. I shared my concern with my sister. "Dr. Kline worried about just this type of 'sour' situation. I don't want Stacey to leave this hospital with the weather like this. *It is not safe.* Sis," I pleaded. "Please call Sandy again. Tell her I changed my mind. I do not want them to move her under these conditions. Guard her bed. Don't let them take her. I need to speak with Dr. Kline—to find out if he still thinks it's safe to move her."

Without my permission to transfer, air-transport would have to head back to Denton.

I ran to find Dr. Kline. Within minutes, I located him in his office. My voice trembled as I spoke. "I'm afraid for Stacey to fly with all the air turbulence and lightning. Should I let them move her? Will she be all right?"

He assured me, "Air-transport will have a full crew aboard with equipment to handle any problems they face. They have an intensive care unit with them. The helicopter has the same equipment as the hospital. They can take care of her."

Relieved, I stopped only long enough to take a deep breath and hurried back to Stacey's side.

My sister called Sandy again. "She's okay. They can come and get Stacey. We'll leave now and meet you at Greyson. It's raining hard. It will take us awhile."

Meanwhile, the storm grew in intensity and now posed a daunting threat to the helicopter midflight. The crew called Hobson, telling them of the dangerous weather development. They couldn't land on the Hobson helipad. They might need to turn around again because of the electrical storm.

In the meantime, Ronnie had arrived at Greyson. If anything went wrong in transport, my husband intended to confront GHP for insisting on this move.

The crew from Greyson's Intensive Care Unit stood on alert, watching for the helicopter to arrive. Sandy's memory of these emotionally-charged moments reveals everyone's mental strain:

> Ronnie, already agitated, paced by the elevator waiting to go to the helicopter pad to meet Stacey when they landed. He heard air-transport might turn around and not pick up Stacey. I worried about his reaction to this turn of events.
>
> Then I overheard Hobson had decided to take Stacey by ambulance, to make the transfer somewhere else. Ronnie fumed. A few minutes later, we heard air-transport took off with Stacey on board. They were on their way.

I wondered what Hobson's nurses and doctors—those who had cautioned us *not to even bump her bed*—thought of this dangerous chain of events. In fact, while in midflight, the Greyson crew decided against landing at Hobson Medical Center. Uneven asphalt waffled the stretch of road Hobson's ambulance took to meet the helicopter. Sections of cement butted against prominently raised seams, bumpy and jarring. The medical staff at Hobson had taken tremendous care to protect Stacey against anything compromising her best outcome. What were they thinking as they helplessly watched the ambulance turn into the traffic?

Years later, when Sandy described the traumatic panorama of the scene, emotion and pathos overcame her. With quavering voice, she shared her recollection:

> When air-transport landed at Greyson, the sky gradually brightened. The ICU nurses took us in a private elevator to the helipad. All of us—Ronnie, me, the whole crew—stood motionless on the pad, our eyes glued to the sky until the air-transport arrived.
>
> We saw the helicopter break through the clouds, hover, and land. People instantly rushed toward the open doors. The crew immediately began to attend to Stacey, running beside the gurney into the hospital. Someone took Ronnie and me to the ICU waiting room where we waited for Nancy to arrive.

Sandy's voice choked and tears flowed. She broke down several times, overcome by the harrowing weight of the memory.

The memory of the day still crashes over me like a flash flood. The car slices through a wall of lashing rain. A deluge of electrifying energy, surging emotions, and adrenalin coursing through my veins propel me as I drive against the torrential downpour.

Drive. Get to Stacey.

Like a boxer, I fight to beat back a powerful, uncontrollable opponent as lightning strikes, thunder shakes, and fierce rain pelts, beating so hard we can barely hear each other over the pounding.

> Lord, I feel beaten, as well—drained. No words left. Until the last few hours, I was so close to her. Now she lies beyond my protection. I know I must gather what dwindling energy I still possess and ask You for strength and help to prepare for what lay ahead, whether hours, days, or months. What's yet to

come? How did Stacey handle this?

Who will take care of her now, Lord? Will Stacey's next doctor have the compassion and thoroughness of Dr. Kline?

Those questions and others loomed before me. The road ahead was difficult to traverse through the driving rain, but not nearly as arduous as what lay before us in the coming weeks.

I never noticed when the rain stopped.

Coping Strategies

- Lighten your load: When friends, relatives, and others ask how they can help, *be honest*! Accept the meals, childcare, transportation, or other support offered.

- Patient advocate: If you need help navigating the confusing, often overwhelming maze of healthcare, contact a patient advocate—a trained professional who serves as a go-between for patients, their family members, and representatives of the healthcare industry. Some patient advocates work independently, while others are available through hospitals and nonprofit and for-profit organizations. They can go by any number of titles, including health advocate, patient navigator, or care coordinator.

- Read Mike Lavere's article, "Changing Healthcare: Will Insurance Companies Dictate Quality of Care?" for an interesting take on the intermingling of today's ever-evolving insurance and healthcare.

CHAPTER 9

Greyson,
First Report

You need to turn everything off. Let her die.

Dr. Barnett

R onnie and I sat in a conference room at the Greyson Medical Center. I had yet to see Stacey. We met privately with Dr. Barnett and Dr. Imber. Barnett, the doctor on call, performed the intake examination and therefore dominated the meeting.

Barnett, a tall, thin man, seemed much older than Dr. Kline. Gray hair framed his angular face. His piercing eyes demanded attention. My first impression of him was rigid, glacial. He seemed to be the antithesis of young, personable Dr. Kline.

Dr. Barnett's manner appeared just as frigid as his physical characteristics. An ex-military man, he exhibited a commanding presence, seasoned with years of impeccable experience as head of Greyson's critical care unit. Barnett delivered his assessment of Stacey's condition without emotion, presenting straightforward facts set against a hopeless, sterile background. I flashed back to Stacey's bedside at Hobson when the chief neurosurgeon had callously dismissed our daughter's life.

Pokerfaced, Dr. Barnett reiterated the facts we knew all too well. "A craniectomy has been performed. Dr. Kline removed a portion of the patient's skull on the right side. He may not have been able to close it because of the brain's swelling. This section of the skull is still off. Hobson's reports indicate trouble with intracranial pressure during surgery and trouble maintaining her pressure at normal levels. The patient's brain has been lacerated.

"This patient is still alive only because Hobson intervened. They removed part of her skull and administered substances to counteract the natural response to such an injury. If they had stayed out of it, she most likely would have died within hours. Her intracranial pressure is no longer relevant. The bleeding's not an issue."

Astonished, I wondered why. What had happened to change things since Dr. Kline's last exam only hours ago?

Dr. Barnett presented his dismal report with less compassion than one recites a list of items to purchase at the hardware store. Each word assaulted me like projectile vomit. I tried to deflect his words, to shut him out of my mind.

He continued his brief synopsis and then concluded, "You need to shut everything off. Remove life support. Your daughter's condition is not going to change. Not ever. What you see is what you get. You need to turn everything off. Let her die."

Did he really say that?

My thoughts seethed just beneath the surface. *Stop. Enough!*

Only a few hours before, Hobson had been fighting hard for her. Dr. Kline continued to hold out hope for Stacey. He had other patients with similar injuries. Those people might not have been the same as before, but they lived—and regained some function. We did everything we could to give Stacey that chance, if there was any chance.

Let me out of here. How dare this man speak of shutting everything off and letting her die?

Dumbfounded and deflated, I waited for the doctor to finish his apocalyptic proclamation and release us from the private torture session. He hadn't finished talking. I had finished listening. I don't know how I kept from screaming at Dr. Barnett. Ronnie's presence probably reined me in. I thought I might lose my mind.

Definitely unconvinced, I rejected the validity of his grim assessment. Regardless, God could still perform a miracle in our daughter.

Even with years to separate myself emotionally from the meeting with Dr. Barnett, the first wave of unbelief and shock still washes over me. Barnett seemed unnecessarily unfeeling, detached. How does one isolate emotions from such a barren, hopeless prophecy spoken over her child?

Leaving the conference room, I vowed, "I never want to see that man again. Ever! He *will not* take care of our daughter."

Somehow, I got the mistaken impression Ronnie had accepted Barnett's prognosis. I didn't realize until years later, when Ronnie finally began to share his perspective of this experience, how deeply Dr. Barnett's declaration wounded him. Dr. Barnett's assessment and recommendation repulsed Ronnie as it had me. The ultimatum the doctor presented tortured both of us.

I stubbornly held on to Dr. Kline's departing words, optimistic words, words Ronnie never heard. This possibility of a positive outcome still reverberated within me, continuing to ring in my ears: "She can still come through this."

I could not accept Barnett's cold pronouncement. Not ready to take the step he prescribed, I just couldn't give up. Instead, I dug deeper. Like a soldier digging, scratching, and clawing in the trenches, I dug down for deeper faith in God's power to save our daughter.

As it turned out, Barnett never would care for Stacey over the long term. He headed Greyson's critical care unit, not trauma. Dr. Imber, also a critical care specialist and surgeon, directed the trauma unit. Although not on call when Stacey arrived at the hospital, Stacey's care naturally fell under the direction of Dr. Imber, to whom she'd been assigned.

I clung to the belief that Dr. Barnett had been premature in the delivery of Stacey's death sentence. I thought God might open the eyes or heart of another physician who would throw us a lifeline of hope. I requested another meeting.

Within twenty-four hours, Ronnie and I met with both Dr. Barnett and Dr. Imber a second time. I wanted others to hear this report, others who would listen and take in something I might miss. I needed them to stand with me in prayer. I needed those who, regardless of Barnett's hopeless prognosis, would not give up on Stacey—or God. Several family members agreed to be present at this second meeting.

This time Dr. Imber took charge of the meeting. Immediately impressed with his patience and kindness, his attitude and demeanor calmed me. I strained to hear every word the doctors spoke as they reviewed their latest evaluations, desperate to understand and process the information. Dr. Imber and Dr. Barnett *both* voiced their agreement. Upon further examination and the newest reports from the Greyson team, they agreed the prognosis for Stacey was, indeed, bleak. The doctors described the best scenario: "The most you can hope for is she'll be able to handle her own saliva someday."

I could see the shock on my family members' faces.

God, give me something to hold onto—someone who will stand with me. The doctors have given up. I think Ronnie agrees with them. It hurts to think some of my brothers and sisters might be giving up, too. I can't fight this alone.

Ronnie asked a series of questions and then left the meeting abruptly. My brother, Steven, and his wife, Sandy, remember how Ronnie looked as he walked out. "Ronnie came out upset and stone-faced with his only words, 'I'm leaving.' He walked straight out of the hospital and went home."

Years later, I asked my brother Steven what he remembered regarding this meeting. He told me, "I thought I understood why Ronnie left so suddenly. This clinched it for me, too. I thought, 'They need to end it. Ronnie felt it was over, and it was time to end it. I agreed.'"

Unfortunately, for years, I, too, mistakenly believed Ronnie had given up at this point. I felt isolated and alone over the course of the next few weeks as I stubbornly refused to consider ending my daughter's life.

I leaned even harder on my faith, and my siblings and I began to pull away from Ronnie. My husband felt I had inappropriately invited others into extremely personal matters. He had no need or desire to have others involved in our decisions. Years passed before Ronnie and I really understood each other's perspective and needs.

Following the first two conferences at Greyson, Ronnie rarely visited Stacey with me during the daytime but saw her in the evening after work. We sat together at her bedside only a few more times. Over the next weeks, although he tried to get updates on her condition, he received little information from Stacey's doctors. I tried to tell Ronnie what I learned each day, but because I didn't understand most of what I heard (not until years later when I interviewed the doctors), my communication failed to keep him adequately informed.

On September 9, Greyson Medical Center took another CT scan. The scan showed the large hole with a collection of CSF fluid (cerebral spinal fluid) outside of the brain. Dr. Imber's team confirmed Stacey's brain had actually herniated, (squeezed down through the little hole), resulting in the death of brainstem tissue. Not only did the brain herniate through the hole, but also to the tentorium[16] or fibrous layer. The scan revealed low attenuation value, meaning either edema (intercellular fluid in the tissue), or necrotic tissue (dead tissue), was present on the right side. Although Dr. Kline had hoped the remaining brain tissue would stabilize, Greyson's team discovered more had died.

Dr. Imber informed us of a blood clot on the left side, which he said Hobson's records had previously noted. As with the right side of Stacey's brain, the left showed low-density areas, edema, and water density as opposed to living tissue. In addition, the midbrain, thalamus, and brainstem showed possible infarct. (Infarction is the lack of blood flow to the point of death of living cells and tissue). The brainstem also showed evidence of bleeding, a blood clot (hematoma), and edema.

With the exception of the cerebellum, this CT scan showed abnormalities throughout the brain. The cerebellum, a comparatively small part of the brain, lies at the base of the skull behind the pons and medulla and controls motor coordination. Unfortunately, all messages sent and received by the cerebellum need to travel on neural pathways—most of which were either damaged or destroyed.

At the time, I didn't realize nor understand the significance of this new evidence any more than I had understood Dr. Kline's reports. This CT scan presented concrete evidence of the severe damage Stacey's neural pathways had sustained throughout her brain and even into the brainstem.

Dr. Kline had hoped the intracranial pressure monitor gauge had simply shifted and produced inaccurate readings. The Greyson doctors somehow knew what Dr. Kline had not yet confirmed or conceded. However, at that point I couldn't understand, or wouldn't accept, that Dr. Kline's optimism had been proven wrong. In fact, based on what would happen over the next weeks, the readings had most likely been accurate and were now confirmed by Greyson's grim assessment. The monitor registered catastrophically high readings of pressure, which continued to build and cause even greater damage than Dr. Kline had envisioned.

Despite the exemplary care Stacey had received thus far, the mounting number of tests and scans showed, regardless of exhausting every possible medical treatment, her brain simply couldn't compensate for the intrinsic damage throughout. Thus, her body now responded to the residual effects of the devastating shock. The destructive results were evident to Greyson's medical staff.

I viewed this information and evaluated it through the lens of an untrained eye—and the unrelenting hope of a mother's heart. Although it registered in my mind, I saw only our injured daughter. I knew she still had some brainstem function. She still responded to stimuli. Those meager facts gave me hope that someday her brain might repair itself, and she would come back to us. Actually, Stacey's shallow breathing and posturing indicated extreme damage within the lower brainstem. However, I didn't understand that her breathing problems and those postures meant *irreversible loss of brain function.*

All through September, tests and physical exams revealed more damage as her body struggled to fight infections and overcome the results of the trauma. What remained of the pathways of Stacey's damaged brain cells became an impassable maze.

As the days turned into weeks, my path through this experience grew more and more indiscernible.

Coping Strategies

- Be assertive: If communication with the doctor assigned to your loved one is strained, ask for a different caregiver.

- Listen carefully: When meeting with medical staff, it helps to have another person with you to hear reports, ask questions, and take notes.

CHAPTER 10

Walking in the Light

We cannot capture God. He captures us.

P lease, Lord, I need some direction to follow your path!

All through September of 1993, this plea resounded in my head. It rushed through my soul like the roaring of a mighty waterfall for months, years.

I faced the stark reality of life and death. Life had taken a deadly twist. Powerless to take hold of the future, I could neither foresee nor control what would occur in the next isolated evanescent moment— let alone over the unfolding, unforeshadowed months.

Where's the Light to direct my uncertain steps? Where's the Counselor to guide me? The One in whom I live and breathe? (Acts 17:28).

Where are You, God?

Terror ripped away my daily awareness of God's presence. My desperate petitions before God produced no instantaneous revelations, only faint whispers, barely discernible. The answers came in the form of small, sometimes minute reminders of His magnitude. His quiet expressions of love and concern came to me clearly one misty morning while driving down the mountain road connecting my present home to the tiny village of my birth during one more trip to the hospital where Stacey lay comatose. Upon that quiet country road, He exquisitely defined His Presence in, and direction for, my life's path.

The road coils along the mountain, down into the bowels of the hollow, twisting and turning. No symmetry. Never an end in sight. Never a straight stretch to glimpse what lay ahead.

Lord, I'm losing it. Show me the way through this? What's ahead for Stacey? For me?

Grass grows between the tire tracks marking this well-worn path. A sign at the entrance warns travelers: "No Winter Maintenance." The exquisite beauty of this connecting path belies the impending treachery when freezing rains ice over the weatherworn rivets of deep, muddy ruts. Nevertheless, this fall day, the Lord adorned the sienna-barked trees with every hue of orange, yellow, and red to majestically display their grandeur before retreating into winter's long, grey rest. The morning mist hung suspended in the cool air, interspersed with the prior evening's heavy dew, and dripped from bejeweled trees.

The Master's hand brushed across the landscape. He painted His living canvas, creating the appearance of a Monet masterpiece—His medium, the earth; the vapor, the water. Not simply a replica or representation of beauty, God unveiled Himself with flawless perfection through His creative excellence.

With purpose, He melded elements at the peak of life with those soon to return to the earth from which they first sprouted. Bereft of spring's fiddleheads and furled fronds, mature ferns now graced the ground while only paper-thin memories remained of summer's brightly arrayed wildflowers. Rotting trunks of fallen trees that once provided shade dropped depth into the mural. Draped and damp, the fading undergrowth melted into the blazing fiery fall foliage. One season blended into the next.

Enshrouded by the fog, I inched forward and felt my way through a dense and drippy veil. The unimaginable had become the routine. Day after day, I made this trip to the hospital, sat and waited for the doctor, and hoped and prayed for change or improvement. Our daughter's life was fading away like one who disappears in clouds of mist.

What did her future hold? Hers, mine, ours?

My breath caught in my throat.

Then I glimpsed, wide-eyed, the lodes of light deposited on the course-way like veins from heaven to earth. The beams appeared before me with defined substance. I reasoned if I ventured from the car and enveined myself in the God-path, I could touch the light. From that great gaseous ball of fire millions of miles away, The Creator, who calls Himself "The Light," bent a ray perfectly, then sent the luminescence to intersect my path.

God exists outside time and space. He chose a particular point on the continuum of time, a specific site within the expanse of His created universe, to imprint His Presence upon my finite mind.

He spread the beam before me. I knew. Though unseen, He is real, as real as the sunlight He sends to illuminate the path before me. Each evening He causes the sun to set beyond my view. He lifts this same incandescent globe to rise over the horizon of another soul, half a world beyond my sight. This moonless night would end. In the meantime, God etched His abiding Presence upon my heart and embedded His healing Presence in the fissure of my soul.

We cannot bottle up sunlight. We cannot capture God. We can't hold onto Him as a child clings to his mother's hand. God captures us.

This particular morning for those sacred moments, God removed the ethereal veil hiding His constant vigilance. I paused to soak in the Son, to let Him soak into me, to saturate me with His Spirit. Although I felt alone, He reassured me of His presence. He walked this path with me.

A precious truth I had known as an adolescent became all the more clear to me that day: I must not fix my eyes on the visible—the glaring grit of life and death blinding me to His presence. I must focus on the unseen: God and His promises. God, the blessed Controller of all things, promised to be with me always. He would work this out for my good and for His glory. With His God-lens, I could see through this menacing night wherein death interposed itself over life.

Falling leaves do not herald the end—only an interlude—a necessary passing, which makes possible new spring growth. Some things God allows, even *intends,* to perish. He revealed that segment of His master design in the decomposing leaves carpeting the forest floor before me. Their glorious color would soon fade and freeze into winter's ice and snow. Would Stacey's shell soon lie beneath earth's frozen terra?

Our earthly bodies, once vibrant and strong, give way to frailty and decay. Yet God creates our soul and spirit to endure, to soar with Him. Like an old garment that has served the wearer's purpose, one day, His appointed day, He exchanges the former for something far better. He causes new growth. Rebirth. Life and death are in His hands, and in each, He has a plan encompassing new life—a springtime for the soul.

Lord, please, tell me Your plan for Stacey.

He offered no answer.

Instead, He strengthened me and empowered me through His Word. The psalmist says of God:

You are the same,
And Your years will have no end.
The children of Your servants will continue,
And their descendants will be established before You.
(Psalm 102:27–28)

Mining God's Word for His promises, my tumultuous thoughts found solace and rest, convinced that Stacey rested safe with Him. Though I didn't know God's plan, He promised He would restore my joy.

How could I, a mere mortal, comprehend His grandeur, His sovereignty, His good plan? He was. He is. He will be. I am vapor, for now skin-clothed and bone-corseted. The scene displayed before me enlivened with His Presence. It magnified His omnipotence and dwarfed my present reality. This earth-worn covering would turn to dust. My soul and spirit would live with Him forever. He would clothe Stacey—and me—in eternal wraps. For the present, He enfolded us with His wings. His righteousness covered us.

My spirit soared. I raised my anthem of praise in harmony with trilling birds, swaying trees, and a babbling stream. Not subject to the seasons of this life, God never changes. God is Life, and in Him, we have all our being. His love never fails. God scatters darkness. He is the Light of the world.

When I focused my attention on God and trusted Him, He kept me in perfect peace. My roots grew deeper into Him, and I drew nourishment from Him. I thanked Him for the gracious reminder of His Presence and drove on.

Coping Strategies

- Take care of yourself: Eat and drink healthy foods and beverages and make time to breathe, walk, and rest. Relaxation techniques may reduce stress. Listen to what your inner self is telling you. Stay connected with the person(s) or strategy that provided the strength to endure past trials.

CHAPTER 11

The Beginning
of the End

The thread of hope unraveled.

The decisions before me far outweighed any I had ever encountered before. One of Stacey's nurses at Hobson advised me soon
after her accident, "Write out your questions for the doctors in advance." As this experience continued to unfold, this advice became
even more important. I also started to journal the doctors' responses
along with those of counselors and pastors. Journal entries helped
me reconstruct the experience and added cohesion. Much of this
book draws from a compilation of those scrawled notes and of my
conversations with others.

While September's leaves turned color and passed their peak of
beauty, we watched Stacey slowly fade away.

Our daughter had received the most advanced medical treatment available from the moment the first responders arrived at the
site of the accident. Now, many weeks later, on September 22, Dr.
Clayton administered yet another highly comprehensive battery of
neurological exams. These diagnostics involved extremely invasive

procedures. For a person equipped with normal response levels, the tests would have initiated pain. Yet, Dr. Clayton assured me, "Your daughter felt nothing."

Nevertheless, for those who administered the stimuli and observed the testing, it had been brutal, albeit necessary. The medical team used this data to determine the extent of brain damage and gauge the degree of response, if any. Although Dr. Clayton had not wanted me to be present, he allowed my brother-in-law, Pastor John Gray, to be in the room.

John remembered:

Dr. Clayton covered Stacey with electrodes and needles. She didn't respond to anything.

We had all prayed and fasted before these tests. An earlier exam showed she had only about 50 percent of active brain left. Now she had even less, perhaps 15 to 20 percent. Dr. Clayton explained Stacey would be in a vegetative state[17] the rest of her life. She would not even be aware people were taking care of her.

As a pastor, I wanted to see God heal her. Now I understood God had another plan. I knew in my heart what I would want if I were in Stacey's condition: to be with Jesus. I felt we were holding her back from Heaven. I felt selfish for keeping her here—wanting her to remain with us.

Later that day, Dr. Clayton met with me. His head hung wearily as he told me what the tests confirmed. He had exhausted his medical arsenal of diagnostic procedures. Regret saturated with empathy spilled out as he stood at the foot of her bed, holding his scribbled notes. With his trained eyes fixed on the pages of technologically generated data, he almost apologetically displayed slides of the latest images of Stacey's brain. The computerized axial tomography (CT scan) detected acute bleeding.

Visibly emotional, he explained, "Stacey could 'live' like this, in a persistent vegetative state, but there isn't any chance for recovery of meaningful neurologic function. She's not getting better. She has less brain tissue than when she came to us from Hobson—and what's left continues to die and be replaced with fluid. The prognosis for any meaningful recovery is grim."

More than thirty days had passed. Enough time—enough tests. This report convinced me Stacey would never wake up without God's miraculous intervention. It had taken me several weeks to accept what Dr. Barnett had first said on September 9: "Hopeless for a significant recovery." I could no longer deny the truth as Dr. Clayton's grim words repeated those of Dr. Barnett almost verbatim.

Other neurological tests yielded no indication of brain function. Exams showed Stacey's pupils were fixed, non-reactive. The absence of this oculocephalic reflex[18], sometimes referred to as "dolls eyes," where normally the eye moves to maintain forward gaze in response to neck rotation, carried a very poor prognosis. In fact, she exhibited no visual response to any stimuli, even to light, indicating tremendous brain damage.

Coloric reflex tests[19], where the physician irrigated her ears with cold or warm water or air, likewise presented no response. The absence of these responses further validated Stacey's poor prognosis. Dr. Clayton's neurological exams had empirically proven Stacey felt no pain.

I didn't want to put her through any more of these extremely invasive procedures if not necessary. Yet, in spite of all the evidence before me, I needed more input in order to make that decision.

Gary Levine, my brother-in-law's nephew, was a respected neurosurgeon, who worked in the trauma unit of a prestigious New York City hospital. I asked him to review Stacey's case.

Desperate for every possible resource of wisdom, I spoke with others whose loved ones had experienced brain trauma, even some who had been in comas themselves. Ronnie didn't want to hear any of these stories. My hope rose, then fell, time and again. In every instance, there were significant differences in Stacey's injury as compared to those with whom I spoke, differences indicating Stacey had far less chance of recovery.

Within a few days, Dr. Levine called. His brief report, precise and to the point, reiterated the earlier evaluation: "… severe brain damage. The exams showed an extensive amount of 'infarcted' degenerated brain tissue. Dead brain tissue cannot grow back."

"Dead brain tissue cannot grow back." Those six words struck me like a slap in the face. Jolted, I finally woke up to the harsh reality. Stacey was not coming back. Ever.

That truth marked the beginning of the end.

A few days after Dr. Levine's assessment, Greyson ran further exams, which showed even more loss of viable tissue and function—irrefutable persuasion of the futility of pursuing any further invasive procedures. The thread of hope unraveled as evidence promising a positive outcome for Stacey obliterated.

All my hope centered on Dr. Kline's optimism: "The brain can make new neurological connections where old ones have been destroyed." My ears and my mind could not entertain any other alternative. All this time I had believed her brain had the capacity to repair itself to a much greater degree than actually possible. Suddenly, Levine's words, so straightforward, penetrated my resistant mind. Stacey's body could not regenerate brain tissue from that which was nonexistent.

When I interviewed Dr. Imber in 2009, sixteen years after Stacey's accident, he observed, "Stacey had no brain tissue left. That's the point; there was none left for cognition, the cortex was gone, and the main frontal and temporal lobes … gone."

———

Even after years to process this medical information, I struggle to absorb its meaning. With her brain so irreversibly decimated, how did she continue to breathe? It doesn't seem possible.

I studied the meaning of the visceral term "brain dead" until I finally understood, at least to a small degree, the delineation of brain death. With the advance of artificial respirators and cardiopulmonary bypass machines, the parameters for defining brain death "have made cessation of heartbeat no longer an adequate definition of death and have switched the emphasis to cessation of brain function."[20]

American neurologists, Fred Plum and Jerome B. Posner, further delineate between cerebral death and irreversible coma:

> Cerebral death occurs when brain damage is irreversible and so severe the brain can no longer maintain internal homeostasis, i.e., normal respiratory or cardiovascular function or both. ... Irreversible coma occurs when brain damage is permanent and sufficiently severe so that the individual is thereafter unable to respond appropriately in any major way to the environment. [21]

Not all neurologists agree with these definitions. Morison suggests, "... death is a process rather than an event and cannot, therefore, be determined as occurring at a particular moment." [22]

For our Stacey, the disintegration of the cortex in addition to the absence of the main frontal and temporal lobes resulted in an irreversible end of her brain's activity. She exhibited decerebrate posturing. Plum and Posner maintain "patients who remain unconscious and demonstrate decorticate or decerebrate posturing for more than a week are unlikely to recover full normal cerebral function."[23]

Stacey continued to exhibit posturing mediated exclusively by the brainstem with no meaningful response. Despite the absence of the thinking part of Stacey's brain, she was not considered brain dead. Part of her brainstem was still alive, the part controlling her breathing, her kidneys, and other vital organs.

Stacey's heart continued to pump blood through her body. But was our daughter "alive"? Had all the machines and technology really saved Stacey's life, or had they only prolonged her death?

I believe God places within each of us an eternal spirit. If so, what part does the spirit play in our existence when our body and our mind can no longer participate in this world? Does our soul remain trapped in a physical shell while our organs keep functioning via machinations?

The Stacey we knew and loved would never truly be part of this world again—unless God intervened.

The Lord must have a purpose in this, I reasoned, "Perhaps He still wants to perform an incredible miracle. Oh, how I'll praise Him if He raises her up. Maybe this is a test to try my faith, to prove His goodness. Even if He takes her to Heaven, I am determined to give Him the glory. Perhaps, like the biblical patriarch Abraham, Stacey is my Isaac."

In His own time, God revealed His sovereign plan.

Coping Strategies

- Request input: Medical staff, financial advisors, clergy, certified counselors, and social workers possess a wealth of information and wisdom acquired through years of professional training. They are there to help.

- Request referrals: Reviews from different medical institutions or specialists help assure that all that can be done is being done.

CHAPTER 12

Straining to Find the Path

Teach me, O LORD, how to live by your laws,
and I will obey them to the end. Help me
understand so that I can follow your teachings.
I will guard them with all my heart.

(Psalm 119:33–34, GWT)

For six weeks, we watched helplessly as Stacey bore deep and devastating wounds. For six weeks, we suffered our own wounds. October arrived. As autumn's leaves spiraled downward, so did our Stacey.

Nothing diminished my hope to see her healed or my desire to keep her with me.

Ronnie shared his heart with me. "Stacey wouldn't want to live like this."

"Who would? But she's still alive. There's still a chance. I want to take care of her."

With each new day, my struggle to discern God's will for Stacey escalated. My heart wrenched. What did God want for our daughter, and where did I fit into His plan for her?

Discussions now involved the options of hospice, nursing home placement, or total withdrawal of life support. Convinced, Dr. Imber expected, "If we remove the ventilator, Stacey will only live a few minutes. Her breathing will not be adequate. She will simply stop breathing."

I appreciated Ronnie's presence and his input in these initial discussions. He shared his concern for our other children. They also needed me. How could I care for Stacey and tend to their needs?

Based on the dismal test results, my husband believed Stacey had already left us. He felt sure if Stacey had the choice and could communicate her desire, she would tell us she didn't want to live like this. For Ronnie, only one option made sense: remove the ventilator.

Perhaps Ronnie was right.

Still, each time I saw Stacey, I thought of her only as my child—helpless and hurt. Sweet memories carried me back:

"Oh how beautifully you filled out your pretty peach prom dress this spring.

"Your lovely face. I applied the eye shadow, blush, and mascara. It didn't take much to enhance your beauty, Stace. You're a natural. I loved those precious girly times with you."

Fleeting joy-filled moments.

"Will there be others, Stace?"

"When you fell off your bike, bruised and bloodied, I washed and bandaged these knees.

"What joyful expectation we had before you were born—a new life—a daughter. We could barely wait the nine months for you to arrive. Then the excruciating labor pains. I screamed for hours. You didn't come easily. Finally, *you* screamed. Dad and I celebrated.

"I cradled you. 'Hush little baby, don't say a word. … ' What a blessing you were. You are. When you pass from this life there will be no joy, Stacey."

There would be only empty arms.

Lord, Your plan included carrying her within me while you knit strands of DNA together. For nine months I carried her in my womb while You mapped out her beauty and planned out her days. I nursed her at my breast, nurtured her, protected her. What is it You want me to do now? Take care of her? Let her come to You?

God, You gave Stacey life. I can't take it away. It's not my
right.

While Ronnie couldn't consider bringing Stacey home, I couldn't
consent to withdraw life support. I still hoped God would perform a
miracle. Even if He didn't, I could not believe He wanted me to take
away the only things still keeping her precious body alive. I pursued
discussions regarding long-term care with Dr. Imber and others. Dr.
Imber responded patiently to my questions as to how Stacey would
most likely pass if we allowed nutrition and hydration to continue.
Nothing could have prepared me for these discussions.

Dr. Imber believed that if we had removed life support when she
first arrived at Greyson in September, she would have passed away
almost immediately. His opinion had not changed. The recent MRIs
revealed even more infarcted brain tissue and continued edema.

I decided to consult with Dr. Levine again.

"She's still alive? It's time to begin to let Stacey go. ... Don't venti-
late. Don't resuscitate. Don't treat infections. Continue the tube feedings. Make her comfortable."

Again, I asked others to pray for God's wisdom. I needed to know
God's will. I needed to be absolutely sure. The question burned a hole
in my heart.

Consent for total withdrawal of life support meant the medical
team would not only remove ventilation, but also tube feeds and IV
treatment. At our request, they would treat infections with antibiotics. In Dr. Imber's words, this would "allow nature to take its course,
allowing Stacey to continue on her dying process."

The words of the twenty-third Psalm reverberated in my ears.
I recited them. I prayed them. I breathed them. I groped for their
comfort. I sought their wisdom.

My Lord, which path do you want me to take? You are my
Shepherd. Show me the way through this valley of the shadow
of death. I only want to walk according to your desire for our
daughter and for me.

Give me discernment, Lord. I want to walk in Your will. Please give me strength no matter what the cost. Do You want to take my daughter to live with You? Then take her. I'll accept it. Do you want me to spend the rest of my life caring for Stacey? I'll gladly do it. I trust You, Lord. I believe You alone know what's best. But one thing, Lord: remember, You must receive glory, no matter what the outcome. Otherwise, I can't bear this.

Like a monk repeats a chant, I repeated the prayer again and again and never gave up.

Years later, I read these insightful words of Joni Eareckson Tada. They depict what she learned through a lifetime confined in a wheelchair:

Why would He say no to our cry for healing and relief from suffering? The full answer to that question—and most of our questions—is hidden in mystery, and may never be revealed in this life. Even so, the Bible shows us again and again that an Almighty God gains glory when His hurting, broken, sons and daughters continue to love and trust and praise Him in the midst of heartbreak and loss.[24]

In the midst of our heartbreak and loss, I clung to the promises of Scripture. I sought to adjust my life so my actions would agree with God's will. I realized He gives us both promises and commands: "Therefore, my beloved, as you have always obeyed, not as in my presence only, but now much more in my absence, work out your own salvation with fear and trembling, for it is God who works in you both to will and to do for His good pleasure" (Philippians 2:11, NKJV). Even if I never understood or discerned any part of His purpose, I still needed to act in accordance with His will.

I ached to do something for Stacey. But what?

We had prayed diligently for six weeks; yet, fluid replaced more brain tissue as it continued to die. A sense of foreboding intensified as the days turned into weeks with no improvement. If I made the decision to continue life support, in spite of my husband's resolve, I needed to arrange for long-term care.

Another week passed. Still Ronnie would not discuss any options. I knew if I arranged to bring her home contrary to his wishes, it would cause added strain on our family. However, my sister Bonny had offered to help care for her, so in my mind this possibility still existed, as did the possibility of long-term care outside our home. Even after exploring those options, I felt no peace with either decision.

Although the doctors stressed that Stacey would never regain cognitive function, they emphasized her strong heart. She could possibly outlive me.

One day I sat beside her, stroked her head, wiped away the sweat, and contemplated this incomprehensible scenario. My daughter looked immeasurably more helpless than an infant. At least an infant can cry out for attention. She would never awaken apart from a miraculous intervention from God. I finally understood. More importantly, I accepted it.

What will happen to you if you live longer than I do? What will happen to you when Dad and I can no longer take care of you or supervise your care?

God's calm response echoed in my cavernous heart and careworn mind. *One thing at a time. One moment at a time. One decision at a time.* He anchored my thoughts—even if only briefly. When I remembered God's direction, it made the day-to-day trauma more manageable.

However, before I could take any definitive action, I needed to be certain whether God intended to prolong her life or end it.

Am I standing in Your way by keeping her here?

Anguished, distraught, again I committed Stacey to God.

Heavenly Father, I want to totally relinquish my child to You. I don't know how to pray. You know I want her to live. I want her to wake up and sing again, to go on to college—or even just to be aware of my presence and love for her. I'm trying with all my heart and strength to take my hands off her. I give Stacey to You. Have Your way with her life—and her death. I give up trying to figure this out. I give up my own ideas, plans, and hopes for Stacey.

I trusted the Holy Spirit to intercede in accordance with God's good plan. The Scripture's promises comforted me. I asked God to search my heart, to reveal any interference with His answer to my questions. I asked God to make my own will and desire, my natural desire for my daughter, agree with His perfect will. Then I rested.

Blessed quiet. A few fleeting moments of calm, then. ...

Anxiety crept back. The thief stole my morsel of peace.

God, I never wanted to be in the middle of this! My heart's splintering into tiny fragments. Are you listening? I feel like I'm being pulled apart limb by limb. Every time I look at Stacey, every time I ask for your direction and get no answer, the silence feels like a knife cutting through me. Like I'm bleeding to death, the marrow of my bones seeping out. I want my daughter here with me. Still, I want to honor You with the decision.

Without God's explicit answer, peace drowned in the deluge of indecision and uncertainty. The painful reverberation of the same question repeated endlessly. Prayer dissolved into introspection as sugar dissolves into warm coffee.

If I consent to remove the machines and You choose to restore her, then everyone would witness Your power. Who could deny Your mighty miracle? Many would surely be drawn to You and believe in Your sovereignty over life and death.

If You choose not to intervene miraculously, Stacey would soon come to You. All would see the power of a God who would strengthen and sustain me in my grief. You promised in Isaiah 61 that one day You'd "exchange the ashes of mourning for the oil of joy." You said You'd clothe me "with the garment of praise in place of the spirit of heaviness." Many would praise You when they saw You heal my broken heart and ease my sorrow.

Insidiously, a maze of mangled scenarios slithered into my thoughts. "What should, or shouldn't, I do?" Their images conjured up a horrifying quandary: Was withdrawal of life support the same thing as killing my daughter? I wanted to make the decision out of love for my daughter and obedience to our Savior. Again, as I laid my heart before God, I asked Him to search it for ungodly thoughts or subconscious desires that might lead me to do anything contrary to His perfect will for my daughter. My heart quaked.

Lord Jesus, I enjoy my fellowship with You and treasure it more than any other. Now I'm tormented by the possibility this might be an unforgiveable sin. Will this cause irreparable damage in our relationship? Could this be the one thing You can never forgive? What if it always stands between us? What if we never get past it? What if I never get past it?

Fear stabbed me. Was that my faith leaking out? My trust in Jesus? I couldn't bear the thought of doing something that might jeopardize my relationship with God, forever separating me from my most precious friend. Anxiety suffocates. Worry strangles.

Desperate to hear God's voice, I spoke with many people from all walks of life, from one coast to the other, many of whom I never met personally. Yet, I often didn't recognize God's voice in those of others. The cacophonous thunder of my doubts threatened to drown God's voice completely. I couldn't hear Him weeping. I didn't always hear His gentle whispers or sense His strong hand guiding me.

Only as I look back over those trying weeks from the vantage point of many years, do I now realize how He quietly directed every step of this journey. God bound me to Him in an indissoluble union. Eventually, God made known His plan for Stacey through the results of the neurological tests and exams. Assurances of His love came by way of dozens of handwritten notes and verbal reminders from pastors, counselors, and others. Through them, He gently expressed His unconditional love for Stacey and me.

God declared His sovereignty over Stacey's life through the Scriptures. He identified with my sorrow, mourned with me for Stacey's loss, and mourned for my loss. Whether I realized it or not, because of Christ's provision for my sins, past, present, and future, God would never let go of me.

However, entangled in the throes of the crisis, I had yet to walk in the fullness of such a blessed realization.

Coping Strategies

- Research: In order to make wise and informed decisions, consider enlisting the help of trusted friends and family members to help with research.

- Explore all the options: Look into long-term facilities, in-home nursing support, or hospice, if necessary. Local human resource and government agencies can provide informed and objective insight into available options.

CHAPTER 13

David's Oath

*I don't concern myself with matters too great
or too awesome for me to grasp.*

(Psalm 131:1, NLT)

I finally understood and accepted Stacey's prognosis, but I didn't yet fully understand how to take care of Stacey if I chose to keep her on life support. I learned more every day as I watched Stacey's medical team. Still, they were professionals, trained to care for the needs of a person in this condition. What did I know of such needs?

I spent long hours alone with Stacey, pacing between the four oppressive walls of her hospital room, listening to her breathe and holding her limp hand. Did Stacey have any awareness—even an unconscious awareness—of my presence? Of God's presence?

My raw nerves frazzled like tiny exposed filaments. I couldn't connect with their power source. Or had the filaments shorted, now twitching spastically like our daughter's paroxysmal movements?

"Oh Stacey, somewhere, in the midst of this, I've lost my ability to quiet my soul. My mind won't stop racing. I need to be still. Are you quiet, Stace, inside? I do believe God's in control. He knows what's happening inside you. So, why do I feel this burden to understand everything, to control everything?"

Lord, You call Yourself "The Blessed Controller of all things." I know You are God. I'm not. I'm only Your child. I'm reminded of King David's words, of one of his wonderful psalms:

> I do not concern myself with great matters
> Or things too wonderful for me.
> But I have stilled and quieted my soul.
> Like a weaned child with its mother,
> Like a weaned child is my soul within me.
> (Psalm 131:1–2)

Tell me Lord, why can't I heed these words? Why can't I embrace David's pledge as my own?

Many people commended me for how I handled this crisis. I may have appeared still and calm to those looking at me from the outside, but inside I grew more distressed as I struggled to understand God's will for Stacey and for myself. There were no easy answers. It seemed like trying to decipher ancient hieroglyphics. I grappled to reconcile medical facts with Scriptural truths.

If God planned to allow her brain to continue to die, why didn't He just take her? This question bewildered and haunted me. Author Oswald Chambers in *My Utmost for His Highest* said, "If you know too much, more than God has ordained for you to know, you can't pray. The circumstances of the people become so overpowering that you are no longer able to get to the underlying truth."[25]

Was that what happened to me as I groped and stumbled through the darkness? Perhaps. If only I could have focused on God's sovereignty rather than the circumstance. I relentlessly sought out medical advice and spiritual council, but peace eluded me. I tried to figure out God while He simply wanted to walk with me through this experience, to carry me when necessary, to hold my trembling body, to calm my fears, and to be my peace that transcends understanding.

Our pastor, Will Schultz, and his wife, Ann, visited the hospital several times. Slight in stature and good humored, Will brought vitality to his approach to the gospel. His thick-rimmed glasses, mustache, clean shave, and well-groomed manner gave him a professional, yet approachable demeanor. Will's eyes flowed with compassion and brimmed with tears when he spoke of Stacey's plight. Ann said she and Will talked to Stacey, rubbed her arms, and touched her to try to get her to respond.

One day when he visited Stacey, he brought with him a two-by-three-inch picture of Jesus holding a lamb in His arms while other lambs gathered around Him. Will asked me what I saw when I looked at the Christ Shepherd.

I said, "God must be saying He's holding Stacey in His arms."

"Well that's true," Pastor said, "but I think He's saying something more. Do you realize He's holding you, too? Stacey is His child. But you're His child, too! Either way, God's taking care of Stacey. Trust in God's wisdom and infinite understanding. That's much better than to trust in your work to get it right. It's much firmer ground to stand on God's power to keep you from messing this up, than on your ability to figure it out."

Pastor Schultz's words echoed back to me over the ensuing days, weeks, and years. His "Good Shepherd" picture held more value than I could have imagined at the time. I needed the immediate reminder of God's loving care. Eventually, I would see even more clearly how God had constantly held both Stacey and me in His arms.

Day after day, the doctors questioned me regarding our decision to remove life support or keep it in place and plan for long-term care. Day after day, I asked God to search my soul and direct me. Again, I sought spiritual counsel from several pastors, pleaded for prayer support, and resorted to the medical information as I tried to make this decision.

Meanwhile the communication deficit between my husband and me increased as Stacey's condition deteriorated. We seemed to disconnect even more. I didn't know what turmoil my husband experienced as he faced such hard decisions. In spite of our lack of communication, we finally reached an agreement. Somehow, we convinced ourselves Dr. Imber was correct: "If we remove the ventilator, she will simply stop breathing and die."

After six grueling weeks, on October 5, my husband and I allowed removal of the ventilator and gave the DNR (Do Not

Resuscitate) order. They would not resuscitate or pursue with chest compression if she went into cardiac arrest. Stacey would not receive any aggressive treatment should an infection or other life-threatening situation arise. Acetaminophen would alleviate discomfort.

We made the decision not to remove hydration and nutrition. The doctors were all convinced she would die within a very short time, perhaps within minutes, because she would not be able to sustain herself by breathing on her own.

Ronnie and I believed the medical staff knew what to expect, so we called family members and close friends. Stacey would soon be gone. They could visit this weekend. Many relatives, classmates, and friends, even those from other states, came for tearful goodbyes at her bedside. So many wept while they stood beside her, knowing she soon would not be with us. No one sang silly songs now. Only somber faces of young and old confronted with the reality of death.

I knew God could still perform a miracle if He chose. *Now it will be entirely in Your hands, Lord. If You choose to take her, I know I'll see her again someday. Have your way, Lord. I trust You. I love You.*

On Saturday, six-year-old Laura wrote her big sister a sweet note, placed it beside her, and said goodbye. As her brothers said their farewells, I fought back a flood of tears. We removed the ventilator; certain Stacey would shortly take her last breath.

But—she kept breathing.

I was stunned, amazed—elated. I thanked God. *This must be a sign! You want Stacey to stay here with me, with us. You're not ready for her to go to Heaven. You must have another plan.*

Part of me rejoiced; yet, another part felt like a lost sheep entangled in a maze of gnarly-twisted undergrowth. I had been mistaken. I had not understood God's plan. I knew God still held control. Had He not completed His plan for Stacey? Whatever this turn of events meant, Stacey remained with us. Nothing else mattered.

———

Within days after removing the ventilator, the hospital began discussions again regarding complete withdrawal of life support or permanent placement other than at the hospital. By this time, the staff only administered "comfort care."

I became lost all over again.

Stacey's erratic twitches had ceased when we removed the ventilator. She appeared serene, peaceful now, but peace eluded me. With a convulsive grip, I took back all the details, concerns, worries, and fears. Again, I picked up the tortuous burden of her situation and laid it on my weak shoulders.

Confined within those four walls of her hospital room, I felt safe. I felt Stacey was safe. Dr. Imber and Dr. Clayton cared about my daughter. Still, the room seemed almost claustrophobic, even suffocating. Or was it just the air? No fresh air.

Maybe that's the problem: the air's so stale. We're all breathing the same tepid air the ventilator forced through Stacey's lungs—the same sorrow-saturated oxygen. If only I could open a window.

My soul cried for release.

My mind? As used up and exhausted as the stagnant air.

Coping Strategies

- You're not crazy: A traumatic event or a critical incident may initiate unusually strong emotional and physical reactions that could interfere with your ability to function normally. You may be in a state of shock. This response is normal. Don't label yourself crazy or weak, but do seek medical attention, if needed.

- Express your feelings: Talking about your feelings can facilitate healing and recovery.

- Extend grace to yourself and others. Permit yourself to feel your frustration, fear, anger, and so on. Don't isolate or punish yourself for your feelings. Realize that others may be feeling the same way.

CHAPTER 14

Walking in the Shadows

I cannot cause light. The most I can do
is try to put myself in the path of its beam.[26]

Annie Dillard from *Pilgrim at Tinker Creek*

October 1993

As August's heat surrendered to September's chill, time and again, shedding pretense, face down, I laid prostrate before God on our living room floor praying and waiting. Stacey's condition worsened, her life was ebbing away. I couldn't see God's path. I couldn't hear His answers.

Throughout October, I walked through the Valley of the Shadow of Death. I felt alone, abandoned and blindfolded. The shadows grew longer, more distorted with each day. My mind wandered back and forth through the deepest, darkest hollow lying between this life and the next, lost in a maze of questions, imaginations, and speculative outcomes.

The unimaginable had become the routine as day after day I repeated the trip between hospital and home. Each morning I traveled down the winding country road leading me to her bedside.

Stacey's evanescent shell lingered as autumn's falling leaves hastened their descent. My spirit, caught in a downward spiral, plummeted as well. Only a few weeks had passed; yet, the road before me appeared even more perilous than before. The twisting and turning of my thoughts threw me off balance. I mustered all my strength to stay focused on God as He led me through this thorny path.

The way was in no sense clearly marked. No straight and narrow path ran through this labyrinth, no glimpse of what good might lie ahead. I tried not to move too fast or fall too far behind my Guide. I certainly didn't want to end up like a lost pilgrim, out of touch with God, wondering, "Where am I? How did I get here?"

Lord, please give me light to see the well-worn God-path You've laid out before me, the path You've stamped upon my soul. It's pitch black here in the shadows of this Valley. Where are the guardrails for the child who stumbles? I'm falling. I'm bruised. Show me a sign, any marker—something—so I know I'm on the right path.

Had He sent me a warning of this impending treachery, some admonition I had missed?

Does God provide "No Winter Maintenance" for His child when he travels this blustery road? Where lies the connecting path to my Savior? *God, please keep me focused on Your saving power and Your grace. Then I can maintain my bearings throughout this harsh journey.*

Had I prepared spiritually to stand firm in the Truth, the truth of God's love and provision? Only time would tell.

Autumn's leaves had reached their peak of grandeur. The kaleidoscope of color suspended on leaves hung precariously from their life's source. In many ways, the scene before me replicated that of a few weeks earlier. The Master's hand brushed across the landscape. Again, He created a living lesson on a mosaic of flawless perfection, using the stuff of this earth: winter's death-promise of spring's resurrection.

The morning mist interspersed with the prior evening's freezing rain and dripped from shimmering branches. Limbs appeared as appendages raised in praise to their Maker. He exhaled. The wind first lifted the leaves, then in one grand finale they listlessly floated from their Heavenly abode to blanket the frozen ground below, to paint earth's floor. The leafy, stained carpet lay flat, silent in stark contrast to the subtle browns of the exalting, yet nearly naked, trees.

I felt naked before God. I groped for the Master's touch, His covering for my soul.

Driving down the barren country road, I hungered for His warm embrace and searched for His purpose in this journey. My eyes now fixed on autumn's mural. Colors muted. Lines blurred. Every component pooled into the next as if the Artist planned the portrayal of the blending of life and death.

The Great Biologist laid out His life lesson before me. I paused to study it. Chlorophyll captures solar rays, using the energy to manufacture the plant's food. The chlorophyll of spring's green leaves, now used up, had splattered the lofty heights with color. The One who cloaked the trees now released the leaves to warm the earth and replenish it. He would use the decaying leaves to bring forth spring's new growth.

God, the Master recycler, had proven faithful in the past to replenish me when I "used up" myself. My reserves of spiritual and emotional energy dwindled, slowly at first, now more rapidly. In this particular autumn of my soul, I struggled to capture His life-giving light. Somehow, in the lengthening shadows of autumn, I lost sight of my God. I knew I needed to stay in His light to survive. Nevertheless, no matter how hard I tried, I kept stumbling back into the darkness.

Yet, on this particular October morning for a few moments I saw clearly: He had inter-mixed these elements with purpose—life and death, human flesh and spiritual essence, God and man. Though I didn't see His purpose, I rejoiced in knowing He had a purpose in this experience. Would Stacey survive? Would He continue to pulse life through Stacey's veins? Were those crimson lofty leaves now floating to earth testifying of His blood bleeding into mine—into our daughter's veins? Were those weeping trees His tears mingling with mine?

Enshrouded in this nebulous veil, I inched forward, cautious. Fear of the unknown obscured the path and impeded my progress.

Stacey's life, as we had known it, slowly flowed away. It slipped through our fingers until all we had to hold onto was a body with no function. Had God already completed His plan and purpose for Stacey and did her eternal soul now rest, encapsulated in a lifeless shell? Did she wait to put on new life as a caterpillar transforms into a beautiful butterfly and discards the cocoon it once wore?

As I drove on, the Master again bent a ray just so. If only—if only I could reach out and touch God as I might this beam of light or hear Him speak as I hear the leaf-rustling wind, the bird's fluttering wing, the stream's trickling water.

The illumination of the human eye, limited in the type of wavelength it can perceive, at times may far surpass the soul's illumination, most notably when this earth's Darkness eclipses heaven's Light.

Yet, for these scarce sacred moments, God spread out the full-color spectrum of light before me. He fired it upon millions of my retinas' sensitized cone cells. Suddenly, breathless, I saw it. The Creator of Light had placed me in the path of the light beam as it traveled from its source to that hallowed ground and back again. He sent this grace-gift to lighten my load, to enlighten my soul.

As each evening He causes the sun to set and in the morning to rise again, even so He appoints to each of us a cycle of time, a span of life. Unlike the morning mist, which dissipates leaving no discernible trace of its past, God's Spirit within us lingers long enough and wields power enough to lift us from this life. The souls of His children become a fragrant bouquet, wafting up to the firmament, filling the Heaven beyond our view, a world beyond our sight.

When, Lord, is Your time for Stacey—that moment You've planned when You'll usher my daughter beyond the heaven of heavens into Your throne room?

Slowly, like watching the sun rise, reality dawned. This dark night had not yet completed God's appointed purpose. Although I couldn't see His "face" in it, His glory shone down upon my daughter and me. God's glory, His holy nature, mirrors the manifold perfections of His intrinsic character. The attributes of God, His goodness, His perfection, His grace, His mercy, His omniscience, His love lightened my load, dispelled the shadows, and illuminated the path before me. Wonderful, soul-comforting Scripture filled my mind:

> And He said, "I Myself will make all My goodness pass before you, and will proclaim the name of the LORD before you; and I will be gracious to whom I will be gracious, and will show compassion on whom I will show compassion." But He said, "You cannot see My face, for no man can see Me and live!" Then the LORD said, "Behold, there is a place by Me, and you shall stand there on the rock; and it will come about, while My glory is passing by, that I will put you in the cleft of the rock and cover you with My hand until I have passed by." (Ex. 33: 19–22, NASB)

In the light of this particular morning, God removed the curtain obscuring my path to Him. He met me in this sanctuary of light and glory. I knew I was not alone. Like Moses, although in this present state I could only possess an imperfect knowledge of God, I could sense His power and presence in this crisis. God showed me what I must do. I must fix my eyes, not on what I could see: these terrible, glaring circumstances, which temporarily blinded me to His presence. I must fix my faith on that which I couldn't see: His abiding presence within me, His unconditional love sustaining me, and His Sovereign hand upon me and upon my daughter.

God inhabits the praise of His creation, whether it be stones or trees—or a "used-up" creature like me. If I could keep my focus on Him, then I could see beyond the shadows and walk in His Light.

For a time, I wandered through shrouded shadows of the Abyss of the Unknown. But then, I bent my heart toward Him. He bent the ray of morning's sun toward me. I declared with the psalmist, "But as for me, I trust in You, O Lord. I say, 'You are my God.' My times are in Your hand. ... Make Your face shine upon Your servant. Save me for Your mercies sake. Do not let me be ashamed, O Lord, for I have called upon You" (Psalm 31:14–17).

Our times are surely in His hands. All that perishes does so in God's time, for His good purpose. One day, in His time, God will restore my joy. He will redeem this tragedy.

The scene before me with the beams of light enfolding me dwarfed the reality of the present ominous shadows of unknowing. I repented at the thought of my attempt to understand the Alpha and Omega. In His light, I saw the skin and bones of my humanity as a threadbare garment, soiled and worn, which will one day return to the earth.

One day, His power and mercy will release my soul from its earthly cloak to live eternally with Him. He will clothe me in eternal wraps, and I'll see Him face to face, but for now, I dwell in the shadow of the Rock of Ages.

Whether He intended to now clothe Stacey with eternity or to sustain her human form, I resolved to praise Him. I thanked Him for the gracious reminder of His presence. I had glimpsed His goodness.

I drove on.

Coping Strategies

- Don't lose hope.
- Focus on the positive.
- Keep believing.

CHAPTER 15

Holding On

*Make me walk along the path of your commands, for
that is where my happiness is found.*

(Psalm 119:35, NLT)

*S*tay within the guiderails, the boundaries. Focus on the good God can
bring from this tragedy. I tried. Lord knows, I tried. How does one
accomplish this goal if lines blur, if the good end seems unattainable?

On October 17, day fifty-four of the journey, I wrote a brief journal entry. It included certain portions of Hebrews 10. I've put in italics the portion of Scripture I recorded in my journal.

Read Hebrews 10:19–26 (especially verse 23):

Therefore, brothers, *since we have confidence to enter the
Most Holy Place by the blood of Jesus,* by a new and living way
opened for us through the curtain, that is, his body, and since
we have a great priest over the house of God, let us draw near
to God with a sincere heart in full assurance of faith, having
our hearts sprinkled to cleanse us from a guilty conscience
and having our bodies washed with pure water. *Let us hold
unswervingly to the hope we profess, for he who promised is
faithful.* And let us consider how we may spur one another
on toward love and good deeds. Let us not give up meeting

together, as some are in the habit of doing, but let us encourage
one another—and all the more as you see the Day approaching. *If we deliberately keep on sinning after we have received
the knowledge of the truth, no sacrifice for sins is left, but only
a fearful expectation of judgment and of raging fire that will
consume the enemies of God.*

My journal entry for that day ended with the following remarks:
" ... I did not deliberately sin. I deliberately sought not to sin but to
act in His interest so I could determine how best to care for our child
and so He might receive the most glory from this terrible situation."

I've always tried not to take someone's remarks out of context lest
I misunderstand the meaning. In the same way, I try never to ascer-
tain God's intent from just bits and pieces of Scripture.

I knew the importance of understanding Scripture in the context
of the entire revelation of the Bible. However, I failed at times to
consider the meaning of certain verses as they related to the whole
of God's Word. Instead, I focused on only a few isolated verses. This
error contributed to my struggle to maintain peace with my decision
to withdraw the ventilator.

———

Now "a fearful expectation of judgment" germinated within me. I
floundered. I sought God's direction for what to do next; yet, my
thoughts were as scattered dry leaves, tossed about by the wind. I
spoke with counselor David Magreety. I poured out my heart, my
confusion to him:

I'm overwrought with the fear of making a decision contrary
to God's will. Fear I'll do the *wrong* thing makes me powerless
to do anything. I feel like Satan's taking full advantage of my
fear and my confusion. It's paralyzed me to make any decision.

The Scriptures bring temporary comfort and clarity, but
then they seem to turn on themselves and only confuse me
with conflicting messages. I'm tormented by these thoughts
every waking moment and into my restless nights.

I talk to God, I ask Him for direction. He doesn't seem to answer. At least, I can't hear Him. I feel like I've been walking in the light of His truth all my years—until now. Now I feel like I'm walking in darkness, and no matter how I try, I can't figure out God's will in all of this.

After unburdening my heart to Mr. Magreety, my spirit quieted within me for a few precious moments. I listened. He gave me godly counsel and a few concrete steps to take so I could find God's path through the chaos: "Write out, not the reasons for the decisions you must make, but an understanding about the decisions. God does not use guilt or separation to manipulate or lead. God leads by love. He knows what He's going to do. God does not manipulate or coerce us."

His words, like a healing balm, soothed the restlessness within me, helped to steady me, restored my sanity, and reassured me.

"You're right, David. God is in control. He has a plan and a purpose, and I just need to believe He's carrying it out even if I can't see it. I know, deep in my heart, ultimately, God had a good plan for Stacey, for me to give us both a future and a hope" (Romans 5:1–5; 2 Corinthians 4:6–18).

David Magreety continued:

What is best, right, for Stacey, is what the will of God is. If you pull the plug, life is still in God's hands. To *take* life or to *give* life is not in our power. It's in God's power. The decision for life and death is not in our hands. If we take away the machines, whether she lives or dies, that is *His* will. We make the decision to remove or continue machines, not for life or death.

David's words led me out of my mind's turmoil and ushered me into the loving arms of my precious Savior, to a place where I could again experience His peace. David reminded me Jesus Christ was in control, and Jesus loved Stacey more perfectly than I could ever love her. Those words echoed the sentiment of the twenty-third Psalm. *The Lord* continued to take care of Stacey in ways *I* could not. In the midst of this valley flooded with churning debris of human reason and confusion, God led me to still waters for a few moments of peace with Him. He would not give up His plan for Stacey or for me. The Good Shepherd Himself would lead us through this valley into His green pastures.

I needed not to concern myself with matters too great or too difficult for me to grasp. I needed to calm and quiet myself. For that moment, I needed to know only this: both Stacey and I had been saved by grace, grace freely given.

God had much more to teach me. I prayed for ears to listen and eyes to see.

I was a pilgrim on a journey leading to the very bosom of God. Still not weaned from the illusion of self-sufficiency, I had yet to find full satisfaction and contentment in God and have all my fountains flowing from Him.[27] I would never get beyond this valley to rest in His embrace until I learned how to calm and quiet my heart as one who finds fulfillment in God alone.

Had this journey just begun?

As a pilgrim "patiently traverses the long, thorny, circuitous way of deep abasement, until he receives from God's hand that which God's promise had assured to him,"[28] so I needed to persevere until this trial yielded God's good purpose. I had much to learn before I could presume to speak David's oath before the Great Shepherd and embrace it as my own:

> LORD, my heart is not proud;
> my eyes are not haughty.
> I don't concern myself with matters too great
> or too awesome for me to grasp.
> Instead, I have calmed and quieted myself,
> like a weaned child who no longer cries for its mother's milk.
> Yes, like a weaned child is my soul within me.
> … , put your hope in the LORD—
> now and always.
> (Psalm 131, NLT)

Coping Strategies

- Write out your understanding about the decisions you must make.
- Get clarification on procedures and outcomes.
- Hold on: You may struggle with issues surrounding your belief system or your faith. If questions, confusion, mistrust, anger, and/or disillusionment arise, tell someone you trust. Request their confidentiality. Communicating your feelings with another person or with God will help you work through the pain of this loss.

CHAPTER 16

Heavenly Provision

*My purpose will be established, And I will
accomplish all My good pleasure; …
Truly I have spoken; truly I will bring it to pass.
I have planned it, surely, I will do it.*

(Isaiah 46:10–11)

T hrust into the middle of extreme spiritual, cultural, and moral issues, I found myself in a confusing maze through which I could
not navigate. Everything seemed turned inside out, indiscernible,
like the threads of an intricate tapestry viewed from the underside.

David Magreety used the words "pulling the plug." An abrasive term,
foreign to me. Terms like "right to life," "right to die," and "death with
dignity" never before entered my thoughts. Before October of 1993, I
thought of "right to life" issues only in the sense of late-term abortions.

I have two sisters and two brothers, who are legally blind. I listened while my mother read my brother's college textbooks to him.
I watched my mother take care of my dying father for years, his kidneys devastated by alcohol. Our family never considered the care of
"special needs" persons as something to debate or to question.

Our mother's example ingrained in us a deep devotion to view
life as a gift from God. "Live by the Golden Rule—treat others as you
would want to be treated," she always said. Mother taught us through
example and Scripture to treat all people with respect because they
had every right to live as full and complete a life as possible.

David Magreety's words echoed my mother's reassurance: "The LORD is in control." Still, with advancement in medical technology, in some cases modern medicine extends life while at the same time, it prolongs death.

These days, within minutes of a traumatic injury, we have the benefit of the latest medical and technological advances, involving everything from defibrillators to innovative drugs. We plug into feeding tubes, respirators, and more. We even inject nuclear material into our bodies to evaluate our injuries and illnesses. Yet, to each of us comes a time when even the most aggressive and cutting-edge treatments can no longer improve life. Then these technologies may become more of a burden than a blessing.

Emergency medical technicians prolonged Stacey's life. They resuscitated her numerous times at the accident site, during Life Flight, and again during surgery. Dr. Clayton described Stacey's head trauma as similar to that of President John F. Kennedy, who died soon after his fatal head wound. Dr. Imber and Dr. Kline both said if Stacey's accident had occurred even ten years earlier, she probably would have died at the scene of the accident or on the way to the hospital.

By mid-October, my struggle no longer centered on the medical analysis of Stacey's physical condition. I struggled most with my emotions and spiritual questions. If Stacey neared the end of her life's journey, then in what ways could I provide the most respectful care of her? I didn't know how many more days God planned for her. Still, I wondered what more I could do, what more God wanted me to do, to ensure the best end-of-life care for our daughter. If God already completed His plan for her life on this earth, had He likewise completed my part in her life? Did He plan for me to step back and let her go to Him? On the other hand, did God plan for me to prolong her life with tube feedings and hydration?

Pastor Schultz gave me a copy of a page from a book he used in counseling me. The book, *Life Choices, Guidelines for Creating Your Advance Medical Directives,* poses the question: "If you make

'end-of-life' decisions before death is near, are you 'playing God?'"
The author wrote:

> No. In fact, delaying death when there is no hope of recovery denies death's reality and interferes with the natural life-cycle. Christians believe that life is not taken away in death but merely transformed. It could be argued that those who advocate life extension regardless of the quality of life are the ones playing God more than those who decline artificial life support. Life and death decisions cannot be avoided.[29]

I believed the medical facts confirmed Stacey's prognosis. Too few viable cells remained in either hemisphere of her brain to recover. With equal or greater conviction, I believed God could perform a creative miracle. I wondered how God's words in Isaiah fit into this picture. "My plan will stand, and I'll do everything I intended to do. … I have spoken, and I will bring it about. I have planned it, and I will do it" (Isaiah 46:10, 11, GWT).

Lord, how does this prophetic word make sense in this situation?

Whatever God's answer, I knew one day Stacey would pass from this life to the next. I wanted to do everything to make sure that happened in God's time and with dignity. Each day depleted my energy, wrung out my emotions, and tested my spirit. How long could I continue to wrestle with such questions?

Another week passed since we removed the ventilator. Stacey was still alive—still with no hope of recovery. Her doctors continued to monitor her through periodic exams. Sometime during the second week of October, Dr. Imber entered the room, his shoulders hunched, head down. He walked to the antiseptic-white wall, placed Stacey's latest MRI on the darkened back-lit screen, and flipped on the fluorescent-cold light. I pushed myself out of the chair and pried myself away from her side to view the image.

Bewildered, I stood beside him, desperate to understand what I saw displayed before me. It resembled a negative of an old photograph. Grey, white, and black throughout, foggy, with few distinct areas.

Dr. Imber struggled to speak on a level I could understand. Thoughtfully, with care, he attempted to explain what his trained eye comprehended.

He moved his skilled hand over the insensate film, pausing over certain areas. "Stacey has no brain tissue left for cognition. The cortex is gone. The main frontal and temporal lobes gone. She basically has no brain cortex left. Dr. Clayton's latest neurological exams confirm Stacey has zero higher cortical function." He looked squarely at me. "Stacey does not have any thinking portion of her brain left. Stacey is comatose.[30] We have seen no improvement over these weeks."

Dr. Imber's latest MRI elucidated the hollow cavity in her skull—vacant. His words left my heart hollow. Empty.

His interpretation of the image of Stacey's brain cut through me like a laser of sunlight straight from the burning, fiery ball. When sunlight sears, you just want to shut your eyes. It hurts. It assaults. But I could no longer shut out the glaring reality. Nausea swept over me. I trembled. Yet, God steadied me and kept my wits about me.

Years after this bedside scene took place, when I spoke to Dr. Imber regarding this MRI, he explained some of the terms he used that day in Stacey's hospital room. I began to see more clearly what Dr. Imber saw in the MRI. I asked him if he would have classified Stacey as an anencephalic, one with no cerebral hemisphere. He answered, "Not *quite* anencephalic."

Noted professors of neurology, Fred Plum, MD and Jerome B. Posner, MD, include in their diagnosis of a coma an incapability of interacting with others.[31] Stacey lost the use of her physical senses. She couldn't hear me say, "I love you, Stace." When I swabbed her mouth, the moisture didn't quench her thirst. She felt no thirst. When I combed her hair and wiped her forehead, she felt nothing. She couldn't see the cards hanging on the walls, cards written with love and concern, cards sent with prayers lifted to Heaven. Our bedside prayers fell on unhearing ears. Nothing remained to connect the sound to an awareness of it.

There were never any curative treatment options. We had only to cling to the shallow hope of "wait and see." How much viable tissue would remain? Her fight had ended. Her brain was gone. When would I admit this sorrow to others and to myself? The stark reality required a radical shift in my thoughts.

God reminded me of another part of my daughter: her spirit. The accident could never alter that part of Stacey. When Stacey invited God into her life, He came to dwell within her, in the innermost part of her being, in her spirit. This indwelling of God marked Stacey as God's child and gave Stacey her true identity.

Even if she didn't sense my presence, I believed God, somehow, communicated His presence to Stacey. And so, each evening I leaned over her still body and whispered the name I gave her when she entered this world. "Stacey, I'll see you again, darling. If I don't see you in this world, I will see you in the next. I love you, Baby Doll."

Lord, I believe You're tenderly watching over Stacey. You're taking care of her in ways I never could. But Father, when I placed Stacey's outcome in Your hands—when we removed the ventilator—I didn't expect this. Did you plan this? It's not what the doctors or Ronnie or I thought would happen.

Yet, You knew it would take me until this day to come to terms with what the doctors are saying. You knew it would take this long for Stacey's condition to worsen to this degree. You knew it would take this long to turn my focus away from Stacey's physical condition and focus on her spiritual condition. Her body holds an eternal soul, which now lingers between this life and the next. When do I let her go? How do I let her go?

In my bedtime prayer with her, I assumed Stacey would dwell with God whenever she breathed her last of this world. The thought of seeing her again, if not the following day, then, at least, one day in eternity's future, sustained, consoled, and comforted me. "Stacey, I *will* see you again, if not in this world, in Heaven." I spoke these words to her spirit. I hoped God delivered them straight to her heart. I hoped, somehow, God communicated my love to her, as well. I knew she "slept" under the shadow of His wings. Night after night, I took refuge under those same wings (Psalm 17). However, an even greater test of my faith lay ahead, beyond anything I ever imagined I could endure. God knew I would need unequivocal confirmation of her eternal resting place.

Mid-October arrived along with an unexpected manifestation of God's grace. The gift came by way of a visitor, someone I had not heard from in years. Pastor Hoffman traveled to us from the little home church we attended when Stacey, perhaps eight or nine years old, came to know God.

In the past, God used Pastor Hoffman's ministry to make me more sensitive to the Holy Spirit. The pastor preached the meat of God's Word directly from the Bible, without mincing words. He served a spiritual feast each Sunday. Always on target, God's message pierced us with biblical truth like an arrow aimed at our hearts.

When the pastor came to Stacey and me in the hospital, he came with an assignment straight from Heaven. Through Pastor Hoffman, God intended to reveal His love and concern for both of us—and assure me of Stacey's home in Heaven.

For weeks, friends and relatives had taken turns driving me to the hospital, preparing meals, and helping with household chores. Their prayer support and deep concern for my family upheld and strengthened me as the Lord ministered through them. My close friend Clarissa looked into nursing home care for Stacey. Most days, one of my Bible study girls, a member of my immediate family, or one of my best friends from high school stayed with me at the hospital.

The particular autumn day when Pastor Hoffman visited Stacey and me in the hospital differed from others. I had planned to spend the day alone with Stacey. In the morning before I left for the hospital, I asked Clarissa for another act of kindness. "Would you please call the florist and order a dozen long stem red roses and have them sent to Stacey's room?"

"Of course," she said, without hesitation. "I'll take care of it." My friend never shirked on anything. The roses exceeded my expectations.

When I arrived at the hospital, one dozen perfect, long-stem blood-red roses stood tall and vibrant at the nurse's station as if at attention, on guard, obeying the command of their Creator to impart beauty to His child.

I hurried into Stacey's room, sat beside her, and with brimming tears, whispered, "Stace, I know you'll never see them with your eyes, smell their sweetness, or even feel their velvet petals, but outside your door, on the nurse's desk, sits a bouquet of twelve beautiful red roses for you. They are just to let you know I love you, Baby Doll. I love you so much."

After telling Stacey about the roses, I leaned hard against the bedrail—gazing, searching, and hungering for enough faith to see into her soul. "You're in there somewhere, Stacey. I know you are."

You know, Lord, people are dying of malnutrition all over the world. They are starving to death. Well, I feel like I'm starving to death—spiritually. My faith wavers, and my beliefs teeter. God, please give me eyes to see and faith to believe. Give me something to hold on to.

Looking up, I saw Pastor Hoffman walking down the long, bare hospital corridor toward our room. Without one word, almost reverently, he approached Stacey.

"Pastor Hoffman, what are you doing here?"

"God sent me to pray with Stacey. Only *you* were to be present when I prayed with her."

So God planned this for me? To spend today alone with Stacey?

Few words passed between the pastor and me. God's presence saturated the room. Like a dry sponge, I soaked Him in. The room became a sanctuary. From memory, the unassuming man of God prayed the Lord's own words from Matthew 16:19:

I will give you the keys of the kingdom of Heaven, and whatever you bind on earth shall have been bound in Heaven, and whatever you loose on earth shall have been loosed in Heaven.

Then he asked me, "Do you understand what happened here?"

"Well, I know Stacey didn't hear you with her ears." I pointed to the roses. "See those? I know Stacey can't see them, touch them, or even smell them. They're here for one reason. I want her to know I love her. When I told her, I knew she didn't hear me with her ears. I spoke to her spirit—the part of Stacey that belongs to God. I believe we prayed with her eternal spirit."

I sensed within the pastor a deep regard for the person who remained Stacey, even while encapsulated within her lifeless body. I thought for a moment about what happened, what just now took place in Heaven's realm.

"I see. God has given Stacey an opportunity to tell Him she's sorry, to ask for His forgiveness for the times she walked away from Him and did her own thing. She knows Jesus took her punishment for those offenses. If she had any doubt before, she can now rest assured she will spend eternity with God."

"Yes," he calmly replied.

"And who, when given this chance, would not choose eternity with God? When Stacey leaves this earth, she will go to Heaven."

Just as quietly as he came, he turned, walked down the hall, and left us.

Alone again with Stacey, I paused to take in the miracle, the ministry of the Holy Spirit, the sterile hospital room transformed into the "Holy of Holies." My heart swelled, believing God had visited us with His very own presence and power. Speechless, I adored the Father and my faith overflowed in soul's silent praise. *Thank you, Father, thank you for caring so intimately for my daughter and for showing me how You provide for her—and for me. Precious provision. The soul's salvation.*

God opened the gates of Heaven. Not just for Stacey, but for me, as well. God assured me He had released her from anything holding her to this life or potentially preventing her soul from enjoying eternity with Him. I could envision her walking through those gates. And God assured me I would meet her there when He called me home.

I rejoiced. God confirmed for me, once again, that He had saved our beloved daughter by His grace. Now I could release Stacey to Him.

But would I?

Coping Strategies

- Understand the diagnostics: A good resource for an explanation of radiologic tests is www.radiology.org.

- Keep the eyes of your heart open: Answers to prayers come in many forms.

CHAPTER 17

The Shepherd Leads

*We must run the race that lies ahead of us
and never give up. We must focus on Jesus,
the source and goal of our faith.*

(Hebrews 12:1–2, GWT)

The blessing of Pastor Hoffman's visit and the confirmation of God's eternal provision for Stacey would bring great consolation in the months to come.

Because God's Son lived among us as a man, Jesus Christ empathizes with our pain and our sorrow. Jesus took Stacey's need to the Father who loved her and provided for her more perfectly than I ever could. He also knew what I needed—to draw close to Him and allow Him to comfort me through the loss.

And the greatest loss, the most horrific dilemma, loomed before me: continue or withdraw artificial nutrition and hydration—provide long-term care for Stacey or allow her to die.

This heart-wrenching decision obstructed my vision of the grace and mercy of Jesus Christ. I failed to discipline my thoughts and struggled to follow the logic of my own reasoning. God's wisdom and instruction eluded me when I focused only on that which escaped me. His plan and purpose in this specific circumstance gradually became the center of my focus and blurred my vision of the larger message: His unconditional love and His provision of eternal security through Jesus Christ.

In chapter nine of Paul's first letter to the Corinthians, he wrote of a marathon competitor who trains his body to stay focused on the goal before him. I lost my focus. I tried to discern which direction to take; yet, I let go of God's hand, the hand of the One who had set the course before me. I wanted to be perfect for my Master, but perfectionism of this kind can be an insidious trap. I needed to persevere in this race, stay the course, and keep my eyes firmly fixed on Christ, who alone has completed life's pilgrimage with no mishaps and no sin whatsoever.

Mistaken, I thought God was calling me to a task, a responsibility I couldn't decipher. I needed to lay aside this great weight. In this segment of the "race," He wanted only for me to keep my eyes on Him.

Sometimes we can't make out God's goal for us in the middle of the race, in the midst of the turmoil. Only in hindsight can we discern any inkling of His larger plan. At that time, I could only do one thing—the one thing I must always do, but which became more challenging moment by moment. I needed to trust Him. He had a plan and purpose He was working out. I had to leave the details up to Him.

In Scripture, God repeatedly affirms us. He tells us He's on our side. He would not at this time, or any future time, withhold anything I needed in order to live a joy-filled life. Because Christ's Spirit dwells within each of God's children, nothing can separate us from the love of God that is in Christ Jesus.

When I reached this point in my journey, even with God's assurance, I made another grave error. I began to doubt God's unconditional love. For a time, I started to believe the lie from Satan himself. I began to think I *could* do something that *would* separate me from God. I added conditions to God's love and words of my own to His Holy Word. I forgot we don't merit God's favor and enjoy intimacy with him by our works. It's only by His grace.

I remembered Dr. Clayton's words to me. "Nancy, you think you have more control than you have. It's out of our hands now. We've done all we can."

Yet, I believed I did have control. We had already given permission to remove ventilation. Now the "control" involved hydration and nutrition. Viewed from my narrow perspective, my vision of God's sovereignty blurred. I thought I carried the most terrifying responsibility: "I hold Stacey's life—or death—in my hands. If I decide to withdraw nutrition and hydration and it's not what God wants, I will be responsible for her death! God could never love me the same after that."

The firestorm of October 1993 shot flaming darts of doubt and fear and eroded my confidence. When would I trust Christ? The sacrifice of His life ensured an intimate relationship with God for me—for all time. When would I ask God to forgive me for looking to myself for what only Christ can supply? Only then could I receive His mercy and grace. Only then could I gain a clearer perspective. Perhaps then I could make the decision from not only the vantage point of the context of the circumstance, but also from the context of a less subjective interpretation of God's Word—from the context of God's unconditional love.

I grappled with the hardest questions I ever faced. "Who am I serving? God? Myself? Stacey? I continued to cry out; yet God's peace seemed farther away than ever—beyond my reach.

About the same time, I called David Gates, a counselor from Dr. James Dobson's international ministry, Focus on the Family. I had called Focus several times over the last few weeks and had spoken with the same counselor each time. I explained what decisions my husband and I faced and that we didn't share the same spiritual struggles or beliefs upon which to base our decisions.

Mr. Gates suggested I might ask my pastor for his advice in the matters pressing so heavily upon my heart. He also directed me to Ezekiel 34 where God speaks of the grave responsibility of the "shepherd" to lead and care for the sheep of His flock. I read chapter thirty-three as well and realized the wisdom of the counselor's advice. I learned church pastors are the "shepherds of the flock" appointed by God. They are responsible to lead God's children in His ways, to guide them to His Truth, to intercede for them, to tend to their needs, and to pray for them.

Mr. Gates suggested I consider this decision as a mutual responsibility shared with my church and spiritual leaders. Hope welled up in me when the counselor suggested, "Perhaps God might speak through the shepherds."

Yet, this strategy presented another dilemma. *Could I trust someone else, even someone appointed by God as shepherd over His flock, to lead me in this most personal and critical decision?* I asked Mr. Gates, "Is it biblical? Do I have the right to ask someone to share this responsibility? Shouldn't I carry the burden on my own shoulders? My husband already made his decision in the context of the medical evaluations and the bleak prognosis for Stacey's future. I can't go to him with these spiritual questions. He doesn't think along these lines."

However, anxiety and frantic frenzy bore down on me with crippling force when I thought of holding Stacey's life in my hands. Previously, I had been counseled, "Seek discernment until you have peace." Yet, my thoughts twisted and turned until I could distinguish no path to peace.

Mr. Gates asked, "What does the Lord say to you? Can you make this decision alone?"

We prayed and laid this question before God.

Nevertheless, I still couldn't hear God's voice. With reluctance, I realized I needed help. I decided to speak with my spiritual leaders. God already had prepared the way for me to make that appeal. Dr. Mark Neilson, a respected pediatrician and one of our church elders, and his wife, Mary, visited Stacey more than once at the hospital.

One day as they visited in her room, Stacey's doctors came to inform me of the results of her latest exams. Dr. Neilson began to excuse himself to avoid imposing upon our privacy. I felt an urgent need to have him hear the doctor's report.

"Please don't go," I said. "Someone at the church needs to hear this—to understand what we are dealing with. Please stay."

God graciously provided the support of Dr. Neilson and his wife at such a crucial time in our family's lives. At eighteen, our insurance considered Stacey a pediatric patient. I appreciated Dr. Neilson's ability to interpret the MRIs and comprehend the significance of all the neurological tests far better than could my uneducated eye. I had no idea how important Dr. Neilson's visit and medical expertise would become in the near future. He understood Stacey's medical condition and the situation we faced.

The following excerpt comes from one of many encouraging notes Dr. Neilson and Mary left in Stacey's room after visiting:

> We stopped by briefly to let you know we care and are praying for you. We cannot fully understand all you are going through, but we want you to know we fully support you in the decisions you come to with much prayer and struggle.
>
> We know God will give you the strength you need in the weeks and days ahead, and we trust that, as God's people, we can also provide the human support you need.

Dr. Neilson's personal verification of our daughter's condition became a vital element of how the story unfolded in the days to come. Through prayer and word of mouth, He undergirded and affirmed my devotion to God and to my daughter. He provided tangible support and attested to my genuine search for God's direction.

In a Bible verse from 1 Timothy 5, the apostle describes the twofold responsibility of the elders. Timothy not only directs them to preach the Word of God; he also instructs them to confront listeners with the truth of Scripture. They help others understand difficult passages and apply God's Word to everyday life.

I needed help to discern God's will. Next, I needed encouragement and support to do whatever He asked of me. The Lord led me to three trusted men whom I came to refer to as my "shepherds": Pastor Louis Hoffman and Pastor Will Schultz, both previously mentioned, and Pastor Earnest Sommers.

Weeks earlier, I first shared with these three men what the medical reports showed. When we removed the ventilator, I asked for their prayers and counsel. I remembered Pastor Hoffman felt strongly at that time not to place Stacey in a nursing home but to allow her to go home with the Lord.

I shared with each of the men what both Dr. Clayton and Dr. Imber had said: "If we remove the ventilator, she will simply stop breathing and die within hours." Now, what seemed like centuries later, yet in reality covered only weeks, I needed to call on these men again and, as best I could, inform them of her present condition and prognosis.

With a heavy heart, I asked each man, "Will you bear the burden of this decision with me?"

The pastors agreed to pray and fast before returning to me with wisdom from God.

A few days later, physically and emotionally drained, I mustered what little strength remained and prepared to call the three pastors. Earlier that October morning, Ronnie left for work, as usual. Casey and Laura settled into their normal routine at school. For me, that morning differed from any other.

The empty house shouted Stacey's absence. It felt like years since she filled the house with her music. I felt hollow. Like the bark skeleton of a disintegrating fallen tree. I could hear myself breathing, yet the molecules of air seemed frozen in space, and breath never seemed to reach the deepest parts. My chest moved in and out, but even that effort wearied me.

Depleted, I sat with pen and tablet before me. I glanced at the antique washstand that had belonged to Ronnie's grandmother and remembered. ... *Grammy and Pappy wrote such tender notes to Stacey only weeks ago. Will they ever see their dear granddaughter again?*

Sighing heavily, I dialed the phone.

"What did you hear from God, Pastor Hoffman?" I knew he had taken my request to the Father. I knew I could trust this faithful servant to speak only God's will. Now I hoped with all my heart to receive God's clear direction.

"If there's no hope, let her go."

My breath caught in my chest. It wouldn't move deeper, and it wouldn't escape. I wrote down his words and repeated them back to him. I needed to be sure I didn't miss anything. Thanking him, I said goodbye.

Snail-like, sighing between each digit, I dialed the phone again. Pastor Schultz answered. When I called him a few days earlier, he promised he and Ann would take my request to the Lord. Now he tried his best to help me with his answer from God: "Let her go to Jesus. Allow them to remove life support."

Later Ann told me, "Will struggled for days with your request for counsel. He needed to evaluate the situation. It wasn't something he took lightly."

Pastor Schultz recently took a position with an insurance company associated with our denomination. He called their headquarters to talk to them regarding this case. He asked their advice on how to pray with me and spoke with the insurance company's doctor to get a medical perspective from a Christian position.

Pastor Schultz had no experience in a situation like Stacey's. Many years later, he shared more with me about his feelings regarding Stacey. He recalled the whole trauma as "being very touchy with your husband because he was on his own pilgrimage through this journey. Ron was not on the same wavelength at all. He based his decisions solely on the doctor's reports.

"I felt if Stacey was being kept alive with life support, then that was unnatural anyway. She was alive, yet with no hope of anything coming out of it. If life support had not been available, she would have already died. Removing it brought it back to the natural. Let life take its natural course."

I called Pastor Earnest Sommers last. He was our pastor for a number of years while we attended church with my mother. He knew our family best. Short in stature, round like a teddy bear, with deep, brown eyes, Pastor Sommers possessed a serene demeanor that matched his insightful spirit. He radiated empathy and concern. Day after day, he entered Stacey's room quietly and settled his robust frame into the single upholstered hospital chair nestled in the corner of the tiny room. He fit nicely there. He visited regularly with Stacey and me, simply sitting contemplatively, his Bible resting on his belly, often with eyes closed, conversing silently with His Friend, the Great Physician.

His prayers seemed to lift from the Holy Scriptures and waft toward Heaven like a sweet perfume. His presence did not impose, yet he brought with him the powerful aroma of the Holy Spirit. The compassion and pathos of the Savior intertwined within the heart and soul of this man—strong, yet gentle; sensitive, yet self-controlled.

Now he responded to my request. "Whatever you decide, it will be right because you are not making these decisions lightly but with much prayer and care, guided by love. As much as I can know, or think I know, or understand the mind of God, I don't believe God will judge you, no matter what decision you make because you love God. And you love Stacey."

On that October day, when Pastor Sommers shared with me what the Lord laid on his heart regarding Stacey, He didn't tell me what to do. His thoughtful concern involved relationship—my relationship with God and my relationship with our daughter. He turned me toward Jesus, the One who lived in perfect love relationship with His Father. The Holy Spirit would enable me to see God's will and appropriately express the Father's love toward Stacey. God would show me the way.

Pastor Sommers also reminded me I wouldn't be alone because Christ lived in me, and He'd guide me in the decision by His love, empower me with His Spirit's strength, and one day He'd remove this spirit of heaviness. Most importantly, one day God would exchange Stacey's broken body for an eternal one, brand new and whole. He controlled the timing, and I had to remove myself from the equation.

Many years later Pastor Sommers told me of a time when he had experienced an emotional and spiritual crisis in his past that affirmed God's love for him:

Basically it was depression dealing with guilt, not necessarily because of anything I had done. But I suffered emotionally. I beat up on myself and said to myself, "How can God love me? I am so unworthy." I did not hear an audible voice, but it was just as if God spoke to me, just as plain.

And God said to me: "When *were* you worthy?"

I responded, "Not on the best day of my life."[32]

Though I struggled to be perfect, understand everything, and live a blameless life, I knew I was far from perfect. Christ alone could fully discern the secret places of my heart. He knew me better than I knew myself. Whether God wanted me to take care of Stacey or to withdraw life support and allow her to go to Him, God would give me the strength I needed.

I placed my hope in Christ my Shepherd and walked on through the Valley.

Coping Strategies

- Big picture: Don't expect to know or understand all of what is going on. Try to look at the big picture. Attempting to make sense of every minute detail will become overwhelming.

CHAPTER 18

The Fleece

He shall gently lead those with young.

(Isaiah 40:11, KJV)

About the same time I sought help from the pastors, God supplied yet another resource. Chuck Jackson, a retired college professor, and his wife, Kit, were prayer warriors, seasoned lay counselors, and Bible scholars who attended my church. They asked me several times to meet them in our church's prayer room. I had hesitated—until now when I realized I needed all the help I could get. The Lord often drew Kit to hurting or needy people, especially those with handicaps. Again, Kit approached me, "Would you please let us pray with you? I think we can help you."

When I met with them, we read Judges chapter six. Verse 39 struck a chord in my broken heart: "Then Gideon said to God, 'Please don't be angry with me, but let me make one more request. Let me use the fleece for one more test. This time let the fleece remain dry while the ground around it is wet with dew.'" Gideon put out a fleece to determine the Lord's will. When we prayed and sought God's direction, we thought of putting out a fleece of our own.

Shortly after meeting with Kit and Chuck, I spoke again with David Gates. He helped me put into words my request to God for direction by way of a fleece. We decided the fleece would be one last MRI.

Shortly thereafter, I called Dr. Imber. "Can you please run just one more MRI? I know they have all come back with nothing to indicate the brain has become stable, but I need you to run one more. Then tell me what you see. I need to know if more of Stacey's brain is gone, or if her brain cells have stopped dying."

He agreed to run the test, although he voiced his expectation of seeing no positive change or improvement. I wanted to hear God speak through that test so I remained firm in my request.

In a written prayer, I relinquished my will and laid my fleece before God:

> If You have continued to allow Stacey's brain to die, then I'll take that as a sign from You, God, that You're releasing me from the responsibility of keeping her body alive, and I'm to withdraw machines and release her entirely into Your care as soon as possible.
>
> If the MRI shows brain tissue that appears to be normal, an amount that exceeds any prediction or expectation of the doctors, then I'll pursue convalescent care and prolong life with machines, treatment, and medicines.
>
> I need to know what to do here, God. This is the only way I know of not doing the wrong thing and causing separation between us.
>
> It's all I can come up with, as much as humanly possible, to determine the right thing. I need Your blessing, I need Your guidance, I need our relationship to be unhindered. I love You with all my heart. You are my Savior and my God.

I asked the three pastors to pray and fast again for God to confirm His will through my fleece, the MRI.

Pastor Hoffman responded to my request with compassion and tender resolve. "If there's no hope, let her go. If the same results come back, let her go. You will not be guilty. If you do let her go, you will see her when you get to Heaven. She'll thank you for it."

Earlier, someone sent a comforting note to me: "I have in my mind a picture of the Good Shepherd carrying you. 'He tends his flock like a shepherd. He gathers the lambs in his arms and carries them close to His heart'" (Isaiah 40:11, NIV). The New King James Version of this passage reads, "He … shall gently lead those that are with young." God's Word reminded me of the picture Pastor Schultz gave me, the one of Jesus surrounded by the sheep. Again, the Good Shepherd reassured me that He carried both Stacey and me.

While waiting for the results of the MRI, the promise of Romans 8:27 bolstered me: "For He who searches the hearts knows what the mind of the Spirit is, because He makes intercession for the saints according to the will of God." *According to the will of God.* God would work all this out, according to His plan for Stacey.

———

Dr. Imber called with the results of Stacey's final MRI—my fleece.

The MRI is worse. There's more defined evidence of destruction and hemorrhage. It's basically unchanged as all of the right side is damaged. The left side is not as uniformly damaged, but now there are more defined areas of infarction bilaterally. On the left side, 75 percent of the tissue is dead, evacuated, absent. She has zero higher cortical function, and none of this damage is reversible. Brain tissue does not regenerate.

I had heard those visceral words before: "*Brain cells do not regenerate.*" Those words struck the deepest part of my being, making me want to wretch.

One day that week, I personally handed some of Stacey's records to Dr. Kline. I faxed others to him from Greyson the day before. I wanted to find out what Kline would now say regarding her prognosis. That man had operated on Stacey's brain. He decided how much and what part of her brain to remove. He gave us hope at the outset for a good outcome. Surely, he would have an opinion as to what her future might look like now. He said she might one day walk out of the hospital with some degree of function. What would he say now? Was all hope gone?

When I arrived at Dr. Kline's office, I pointedly handed him the records, then shifted in my seat from one uncomfortable position to another until he finally looked up, and my eyes locked on his.

I saw nothing but sorrow.

I steeled myself. "After looking at all of these reports, tell me what you think." I looked him square in the eyes. "Do we have any chance your first prognosis could still be possible? Can she—? Will Stacey recover any degree of function? Should I still hope?"

Dr. Kline sighed heavily. "This is much worse than I anticipated. Stacey was comatose when she left my care. It's been two months with no improvement."

Disappointment filled his eyes, his glance returning to the notes then to the floor. "She's at best vegetative."

He looked up and before he ever spoke, I saw it in his eyes. I saw what I didn't want to see. "We're getting … to the point. … This is maybe all you have."

By late October of 1993, some areas of Stacey's brain could be seen more clearly than when she left Hobson in September. In Dr. Kline's words, "The CT scans show effuse swelling with some small intraparenchymal hemorrhages, which indicates more blood vessel disruption, more hemorrhaging. There's blood even in the upper part of brainstem, which usually indicates a rotational injury within the skull."

Not until years later in my interview with Dr. Kline did he explain this most disturbing finding: "The brain has two hemispheres. The brainstem point of twist happened in the upper brainstem. Blood in that area indicated shearing. There's nothing you can do for a brainstem bleed because it's so deep and so inaccessible surgically."

My October 1993 visit with Dr. Kline ended with his final assessment: "Stacey is comatose. She has no conscious awareness."

His words echoed those from others. By now they were painfully familiar—painfully clear. Later, when I reviewed all of the doctors' progress reports and my journal entries, I found the slip of paper upon which I wrote Dr. Imber's description of the last MRI and its ramifications. I'm not sure whether I wrote it down when I listened to Dr. Imber review the last scan or when I heard Dr. Kline interpret it. Regardless, my scribbled notes depicted a grim picture:

The last MRI, done eight weeks after the accident, showed even more dead brain tissue. Her breathing continued to be inadequate. She was not getting better. She would never wake up.

Those four sentences said it all. The MRI showed no recovery, not even slight improvement. When Dr. Kline said, "Maybe this is all you've got," I think for the first time, I gave up hope. That man had operated on her brain. His optimism first gave me hope. He relentlessly imparted to me that hope of recovery even when he released her from his care. Sadly, now he took all hope from me.

Coping Strategies

- Seek medical and spiritual provisions: Take advantage of every available resource when making critical or life-changing decisions.
- Temper your emotions with your intellect and spirit.
- Do not confuse feelings with reality.

CHAPTER 19

The Pain of Withdrawal

Would you say we did everything possible for her?

I called Dr. Imber later that day. "Go ahead. Withdraw life support." I paused then barely whispered, "How long do you think Stacey will linger?"

"Given her condition, she'll probably only live a few days, at most ten. Our bodies tend to have several weeks' worth of reserve energy from food stores, but lack of fluid causes problems with kidney function within a few days. When someone is no longer taking in any fluid, and if he or she is bedridden like Stacey (and therefore needs little fluid), then this person may live as little as a few days or as long as a couple of weeks."

"What will cause her death?"

"Probably renal failure. Her kidneys will shut down. She'll most likely become dehydrated to the point where her blood vessels can't keep her blood pressure up. Her heart will stop."

I hung up the phone and cried—long and hard.

When I interviewed Dr. Kline years later, I asked if he would have handled Stacey's care any differently in retrospect:

"Would you have done anything different given the outcome?"

"No, I would still have done everything possible."

"A physician is under no obligation to provide futile medical interventions. Looking back, would you have any hesitation as to how to handle this case?"

"No, I would do it all the same. The initial branch is 'Do you operate, or do you let her go?' If she had been ninety-five years old and in that condition, I probably would have had a heart-to-heart with family: 'What are we saving?' But when I have someone so young, previously very viable. ... No, I still do that, I jump in there. If I don't have family to give permission, I do it under what they call the emergency clause. It's life-saving, so you *have to do it*."

"You felt there was a chance?"

"Especially with her age, I felt we had a chance, and everything else was okay. I'd operate because what's your worst-case scenario? She'd die? You can do your best, and she can still die. But, at least, you know you did your best. If you just give up, you always wonder: well, what if?"

"And you still would have operated, given this outcome?"

"Well, now you have hindsight. Now you may say, 'Was all this fruitless?' I would still do it the same way today. Neurosurgeons do not like to give up. Neurosurgeons don't like to lose. I've talked to clergy and others. I guess because in neurosurgery, you get in there, and we deal with life-and-death situations. You always feel like you want to win."

Dr. Kline continued. "When you save a patient, that's a win. When you lose a patient, that's a loss. Clergy and other medical specialists will say you did everything you could. You cannot win them all. But that's just our nature. So when someone comes in, you don't want to sit back. You don't want to say, 'Oh, she probably won't make it.' Don't *tell* me she can't make it. *Prove* she won't make it. That's the way I've practiced."

"Would you say we did everything possible for her?"

"Yes, we exhausted every possible medical treatment."

———

Following the interview with Dr. Kline, I repeated the same questions in a lengthy interview with Dr. Imber. Dr. Imber more clearly defined the medical terms used in Stacey's prognosis and helped me understand Stacey's condition and her limitations. The following are excerpts from Dr. Imber's interview:

"Stacey exhibited abnormal posturing. Again, there are different levels of response. It would not have been possible for Stacey to respond by squeezing your hand except by posturing with a primitive reflex. Decerebrate posturing, what Stacey did, indicated the whole cerebrum, that is most of the brain, had no influence to noxious stimuli. This is a very primitive body response to noxious stimulation, the most primitive way other than no reaction, as in a primitive organism that darts away in automatic reaction to touch.

"The gray matter on the surface of the brain is the thinking part, the cortex. It controls the high levels of consciousness—the conscious awareness of anger, suffering, pain, hunger. Consciousness involves all cortical function. Stacey did not have any thinking portion of her brain left. Her cortex had been replaced with nonnervous tissue.

"Stacey could still digest food because that's controlled by the autonomic center. But her higher level of sensing hunger or thirst was absent. One hundred percent sure. You have to be aware you are hungry. Awareness is a conscious thing. Your body sends a signal to the cortex, a message saying, 'You're hungry. Eat.'

"Stacey had no pain, no suffering, because she could not have been aware of it. She had no cortex left.

"Stacey suffered a traumatic brain injury. The brain loses cells and can't replace these neurons. Once they're gone, that's forever. The brain will then develop scar tissue where the cells have been lost, which disrupts many established pathways for functioning (thinking, eating, movement, etc.) And during the recovery, which includes our therapy, we try to have the brain reroute the previously learned pathways. Obviously, this is dependent on how much brain is left. If there is no brain near that area, then that function will be lost forever. In Stacey's case, most of the brain tissue was gone. All she had was primarily brainstem, which controls things like breathing, heart rate, and so forth.

"Coma is the absence of response to any stimulation and an unawareness of their surroundings.

"Persistent vegetative state is when the patients remain unaware of their surroundings but may have spontaneous movements, sleep/wake cycles, and some other spontaneous actions that make them appear to the untrained observer that they are interactive. In reality, they are by no means aware of anything around them and not able to interact. This is the Terri Shiavo case, along with many other prominent ones over the years.

"Brain death is the death of the entire brain including the brainstem. This means the brainstem functions that control heart rate, spontaneous breathing, eye movement, papillary response, and several others are also absent. At this point, the patient is legally dead. The heart will continue to beat, and other nonbrain-related activity may continue, such as some spinal cord reflexes, which again can be confusing for the "lay" public. The patient has no ability to breathe without a ventilator.

"Stacey was probably in a vegetative state, at best. Stacey could breathe on her own and she postured … .

"But if you don't have the brain, there is no function. If brain cells are not present, there is no pathway to create. So there is no piano lesson, singing, and so on to relearn a new pathway. That's not possible. Stacey did not have brain tissue to create new neural pathways to help her regain a new Stacey back. We saw the evolution of the MRI and CT scan show that basically the brain was destroyed, and it's not coming back. There were no neural pathways to re-circuit."

This interview lasted nearly three hours, during which time Dr. Imber kindly answered my hypothetical questions:

"What changes would we have seen if we had waited longer to withdraw? Could we have learned anything more from additional tests?"

"If we would have waited two or three more months and done another MRI, CT scan, or EEG, we would have seen more of the same changes. The MRIs show the conversion of tissue that was marginal or dying and then gets replaced by fluid, scar tissue, or other non-nervous tissue. We would not have seen more hemorrhage, just all of the residual after-effects of everything being replaced with fluid or scar tissue. Stacey scored at a level of 'deep unconsciousness' on the Glasgow Coma Scale[33], even lower than decorticate response."

At the conclusion of our interview, I asked Dr. Imber, "Maybe we had given her every chance modern technology can offer. Would you agree?"

He assured me, "I believe we did."

Coping Strategies

- Grant others and yourself grace and mercy.

CHAPTER 20

The Letter

*You can't understand the truth of your circumstance
until you have heard from God. Moses did what God told
him to do and asked Pharaoh to release the Israelites.
The Israelites turned against Moses and criticized him
for causing so much trouble. The human tendency would be
to assume you'd missed God's will."* [34]

Henry Blackaby, Richard Blackaby, Claude King
from *Experiencing God*

Finally, I made the decision. On Wednesday, October 20, I asked Dr. Imber to do the last MRI, which he ordered the following day. On Friday, Dr. Imber called me with the report, and I gave permission to withdraw life support. On Tuesday, October 26, sixty-three days after the accident, the health care team would remove hydration and nutrition. Ronnie and I took the children to see Stacey one last time.

On Sunday, an acquaintance stopped me to ask about Stacey. Maria and her husband had visited Stacey in the hospital several times. At some point during those harrowing weeks, she had offered to take care of Stacey for as long as necessary once we brought her home.

Exhausted, I briefly filled her in and simply asked her to pray for our family. Because she had some medical knowledge, I assumed she would understand the situation. Anxious to get home to the rest of my family, I excused myself.

Beginning the next day, I planned to stay later at the hospital. I wanted to spend as much time with Stacey as possible before God took her. Monday came and went. My heart broke as I thought back over the years we had with Stacey, painfully aware she would soon be gone. I held her hand, sat next to her on the bed, sometimes cuddled her warm body. I wished she could feel my closeness and sense how much I loved her.

When evening's shadows filled the room, I caressed her head, kissed her cheek, and said my goodbye: "Stacey, if I don't see you again in this world, Baby Doll, I'll see you in the next. I love you. Goodbye, Sweetheart." I hugged her, tore myself from her, and then plodded down the dreary hospital corridor. My heart bled all the way from the side of her bed to mine at home, where I finally collapsed, drained.

I held onto Stacey's dear life with all my heart *and* onto God's promise that one day I, too, would pass through Heaven's portal. There my daughter and I would meet again, embrace, and finally live together with God forever.

I knew God could still perform a miracle. I believed He could raise her even yet. He is the LORD of life in spite of death's momentary victory! "Our God is in the heavens, he does all that he pleases" (Psalm 115:3, ESV). Neither anyone nor anything can frustrate His purposes. He will ultimately accomplish His will. He is life. He is strength. He gives breath, and He takes breath away. He is the Sovereign, the All-Powerful (Isaiah 40). These Scriptural truths and the certainty that He held our daughter in His arms were my consolation, my lifeline.

Tuesday morning, I waited, attuned to her every breath. She had no awareness of mine. *She will soon leave.* I was in excruciating pain. I watched helplessly, all the while brutally mindful she would soon die. The accident continued to suck life out of her and out of me.

Wednesday morning, while home in bed, I recorded vivid memories on a slip of paper:

"I feel like a lost sheep looking for green pasture. Where can I rest? It takes all my strength to dress. I will follow my Shepherd through this valley. I will not give in."

I wished I could give our daughter something to nourish her, to nurse her back to health. I ached to turn back the clock so I could see little Stacey running to me—to her mama—for comfort. But my hugs and kisses could not heal this hurt. My embrace could not fasten her to this place.

Long before sunrise, alone, weak, I whispered, "Why? Why this way, Lord?"

She's already with me. There is a reason for this.

I knew He intended His words for my comfort and surety. God held Stacey, secure and safe, forever and ever. I drifted back asleep, consoled. She would draw her last breath according to *His* timing.

I relinquished control and released her entirely to Him. I hoped I did. I thought I did. I knew God could still raise her, still awaken her from her death-sleep. I trusted Him to accomplish His will for Stacey.

I rested and waited for Him to restore the promised joy, the joy beyond the storms and losses of this life. I waited for the Lord to tell me what to do next.

I drifted in and out of sleep.

I had no inkling. No warning. Yet a confrontation as devastating as an earthquake shook just below the surface, so powerful, it knocked me off my course for years to come. Would my faith rupture and crumble as it strained against itself, against the beliefs of others, or would it stand firm? Only God knew if the sudden fracture would be my undoing or my salvation.

I jolted awake. *Stacey's dying. Nothing we did changed that. This could be my daughter's last day on this earth. I can only sit and wait by her side. This pain is an iron vice whose steel-jawed grip is squeezing my life out. I can't breathe. But I must get up and go to her. It's all I can do.*

Although pressed to the edge of endurance, I clung to God's promise to see us through. My brother Steven would take his place by her bedside to read from the Psalms. My sister Tammy and Pastor John were traveling from western Pennsylvania. Their presence would bring comfort and support. I went through the motions, brushed my teeth, showered, and prepared for what might be my final day with Stacey.

I had only partly dressed when I heard a knock. I threw on a house-coat and hurried to the door, where a messenger handed me a registered letter. I scribbled my signature and took the envelope. Glancing at the return address, I wondered, *what could this be?* Bewildered, I slumped onto the couch.

Why would Joni Eareckson Tada send me a registered letter? How would she know how to reach me?

Apprehension and dread darted through my mind. I opened the letter and read these words:

[Stacey] is a young woman with a disability, albeit very severe, and that makes me strongly identify with her needs right now. … Two months in a coma is really not that long—our ministry to persons with disabilities has connected with thousands of families whose children have survived comas, some recovering quite well, and others, surviving to go home in a wheel-chair. A person in a coma is not dying. Stacey does not have a terminal illness. She is disabled. And like any person with a disability, someone like Stacey is entitled to life-sustaining measures. If it were a question of medical treatment such as invasive surgeries or prolonged and burdensome drug thera-pies, these might be considered 'extraordinary treatment.' But food and water is not a medical treatment. It is basic care. And for that reason, food and water is not extraordinary care, but ordinary, something to which any person should be entitled. Starvation is a slow and very painful process.

As I shared earlier, my heart goes out to you, and I'll be praying that God will give you wisdom and direction on this critical issue. I know you want to do what is best for your daughter and what pleases the Lord.

I think my heart stopped—just for a few beats. If that's even pos-sible? The fists of fear and anxiety thumped upon it. Then it began pounding, irregular. First blood gushed through my veins, then crawled, all against my will. My mind staggered. Dazed, I struggled to process what I read. I couldn't distinguish between my spoken words and my thoughts. They pummeled disjointed, erratic, and scattered. The demons set their claws deep.

"Is this really ... happening? Am I dreaming? I couldn't have gotten this wrong. Could I? With all my prayers and so many others, how could I have misunderstood?"

Punishing doubts overwhelmed. Piercing fear stabbed.

"How could I have given the order to *kill* my daughter? How could God have let me do this terrible thing when all I wanted, all I asked, was to do what *He* wanted me to do?"

Uncertainty devoured my faith. My trust in the feeble steps I had taken to ensure I acted only according to God's will crumbled.

My thoughts began to converge on the person who wrote the letter and on her words rather than on the One who spoke through Scripture, through the pastors, through the tests, through the fleece, and through Stacey herself. I reasoned, "This person for whom my whole family feels so much respect and holds in such high esteem says I am killing my daughter. Joni should know what she's talking about. She probably deals with people in comas all the time. She's gone through so much. She's so close to God. She must know His heart in this."

Instead of grasping God's hand the moment I opened her letter, I latched onto Joni's words, her assessment of the situation. Stunned and devastated, I couldn't escape the hellish blast. Where could I run? I had no tears. What now remained of me? A lifeless shell gradually replaced Stacey's once-vital body. Now I, too, became a hollow shell.

The cup God had filled with healing grace and assurance, in one instant emptied. Just as a vacuum sucks in air, toxic guilt, fear, and self-condemnation immediately rushed in. I never anticipated such direct and abrupt opposition with my decision to withdraw life support. Could I have so completely misread God?

Instantly, I assumed I missed God's will. Perhaps at this point, I might have been able to receive God's love and His comfort were it not for my raging predisposition to perfectionism. Instead, I fell into a snare set by the enemy of my soul. I buried myself in guilt. I didn't crawl out of this pit of bondage for years. How could I ever be sure I was walking in His will? Would I ever again experience the joy of His fellowship?

How long did I sit there, frozen in time and space? Minutes, hours? I was unable to walk or even to stand.

Meanwhile, when I didn't arrive at the hospital, Tammy called the house. I heard the phone ring, unconsciously picked it up, intending to speak, but I couldn't. I couldn't form any words, couldn't move my lips—I couldn't move at all.

When Tammy and John arrived at my home, I still held the letter in my hand. Barely breathing, I sat in a stupor, reciting over and over in my mind, almost trancelike, the words from the letter:

> "[Stacey] is a young woman with a disability … two months in a coma is really not that long … a person in a coma is not dying … food and water is not extraordinary care, but ordinary, something to which any person should be entitled. … Starvation is a slow and very painful process."

Tammy sat beside me. "What happened?" She took the letter.

My hand fell limp onto the couch as if one million pounds of force dropped it there. I felt disconnected from my physical body and surroundings, yet weighed down by them.

Tammy handed the letter to her husband and held my hands. Then she pulled me toward her, holding me gently in her arms. I wilted in her embrace.

John remained standing, glued to the words on the paper in his hand. "What—?" He immediately called Steven, who waited for us at Stacey's bedside. I don't remember if John read the letter to Steven over the phone or if he gave it to Steven once we arrived at the hospital.

In shock, I don't remember much of what happened from the moment I opened that letter until the moment Stacey took her last breath—six days later.

The thought of visiting Stacey no longer brought comfort. It tortured me. I was killing my daughter. I found trying to talk with the Lord like I had before impossible. Why would He listen to me now? Why would He even want to hear my voice? Why, when I so completely missed His direction? Why would the Great Shepherd want to walk beside me any farther into the hellish valley?

Despair filled me and clouded my thoughts over the next week. Somehow, I mustered a small bit of courage to ask: "Lord, I asked You to reveal the path You wanted me to take. I pleaded for Your direction. How could I have so entirely missed Your leading? It was obvious to others, but why not me? Why did You let me do this terrible thing?"

Oswald Chambers had written:

In the Garden of Gethsemane, the disciples fell asleep when they should have stayed awake, and once they realized what they had done, it produced despair. The sense of having done something irreversible tends to make us despair. We say, "Well, it's all over and ruined now. What's the point in trying anymore?"[35]

Some may ask, "Why didn't you call the hospital and have them put Stacey back on life support?"

I can't say for sure. I think, perhaps, hopelessness over having possibly mistaken God's answer to all our prayers drained any remaining strength, any initiative to try to figure out what to do next. I had depleted every resource over the past weeks including my mental, emotional, and spiritual resources. Before the letter, I lived the strain, barely holding on. After the letter, I bled the loss, conceding defeat.

Now when I reflect on the preceding nine weeks, I realize I did ask God for His direction and strength. At the same time, I kept a tight hold on my own strength and intellect, my own ability to understand what was happening to our daughter. All had disintegrated. Only ashes remained.

God had given me everything I needed to deal with this horrid experience. He gave me a loving husband, a supportive family, godly counselors, a sound mind, and intestinal fortitude. Most importantly, He gave me His grace to make these decisions and to face the loss of my daughter.

However, little by little, again and again, I set aside the grace of God. I exchanged this grace for an obsession with the circumstance. Although I needed to rest in God in the same way a sobbing child takes refuge in her father's arms, instead I obsessed over knowing His will in this specific situation and my strict adherence to it. I no longer walked in the freedom of Christ. I cowered in the prison of guilt.

The morning Joni's letter arrived, while Stacey lay peacefully serene upon her hospital bed, I collapsed in absolute dejection, dried out and shriveled on my living room couch. Somehow, Tammy got me dressed and to the hospital to sit beside my dying daughter.

I don't remember who took me later the same day from the hospital and delivered me to my doorstep. But I had returned home, alone with my thoughts, indulging in silent panic—no hysteria, no uncontrollable crying. Only quiet terror and deafening desperation. My spirit sank and dejection consumed me. I quaked with fear. *What do I hang on to now? What do I do?* My silent screams went unheard by all—all except my loving Savior.

And then in a faint voice, the Comforter whispered: *"God's grace—God's infinite grace. Be still and know that I am God."*

I responded meekly: *God's mercy—for me, my family, my Stacey.*

I marveled. *God's mercy for even me?* I exhaled. Faint hope fluttered. I wondered if I should mention to my husband what took place that day. I don't remember telling Ronnie that evening, or for months, even years afterward. He didn't know about the letter. I thought he'd be angry, and that it would only serve to put more of a wedge between him and God.

Throughout the day, I suffered in silence. Later that evening, after I'd collected myself, I placed a call to David Gates at *Focus on the Family*. I told him about Joni's letter and of my fear of sharing it with Ronnie. Ronnie already had a problem when I'd discussed our personal matters with my siblings. How would he react if he found out others outside of the family were involved?

Thankfully, David's comments consoled me somewhat but did little to heal the emotional and spiritual devastation:

> What you've done is biblical. I want you to feel convicted in the Lord about this; what we've done is right with God—He honors it. God will answer us, if we ask Him. You have found your peace with God. Be content with God's Word, not needing people to agree or confirm it for you. Rest in God.
>
> Perfectionism is insidious, destructive of grace. You can only rest if you give yourself grace. Don't cut yourself up with thoughts like, "If only I had been perfect."
>
> You have been called to live in peace. You did it the best way you knew.

Even with David's consolation, I still felt at a loss to put one foot in front of the other, physically and emotionally. Shaken to the core, I called my brother-in-law John and reiterated the words I'd just spoken to Mr. Gates: "I don't know what I'm supposed to do now."

John answered, "It's going to go the way God wants it to go." He also gave me a calming Scripture: "Be anxious for nothing, but in everything by prayer and supplication with thanksgiving let your requests be made known unto God. And the peace of God which passes all understanding shall keep your hearts and minds through Christ Jesus" (Philippians 4:6–7, AKJV).

I needed the Savior's consolation, to hear Him say, "I am guarding your heart and mind. Don't worry. Lay down your burdens and anxieties at my cross. I will take them to the Father."

However, I didn't hear God's voice. Instead, Satan's condemning voice thundered. I didn't lay down my burden. I kept it bottled inside me.

Had I turned my ear from God? Had my own voice drowned out God's voice? Whatever the case, I couldn't receive His assurance and comfort because I now walked according to the words of "man."

As God had delivered the Israelites, He wanted to deliver me from my suffering, but I wandered in the wilderness for years. God used the Hebrew's time of wandering to teach them a lesson. Thankfully, He also had a love lesson for me, one that would change me forever.

Coping Strategies

- Recall past victories: When doubt, fear, and confusion enter your mind and you feel like giving in to despair, remember what worked for you in the past. Who or what was the source of your strength? Who or what provided hope?

- Relax and work out: Try relaxation techniques and exercise to alleviate stress.

- Reach out: Family, friends, counselors, clergy, God—who do you have that can help?

- Don't isolate yourself: GriefShare is a caring group who will walk alongside you in your grief. You do not have to go through the grieving process alone.

CHAPTER 21

Saying Goodbye

Ronnie was protecting you. If he hadn't taken you away,
I knew you probably would have held her forever.

My brother Steven

I don't remember sleep ever coming that night. I had dragged my-self to the hospital but didn't stay as long as I usually did. I could hardly bear to be in the room with Stacey. I felt responsible for her impending death. I dreaded it. I headed home, despondent, without hope of ever feeling joy again.

When I walked in the front door, I heard the phone ringing. A familiar voice spoke.

We had listened to her music on cassettes and to her programs on the radio. It was she who had sent the letter—Joni.

She called to apologize. She said my brother Steven called and told her what we'd been going through. Before speaking with Steve, Joni didn't know the extent of Stacey's injury. She didn't know to what lengths I had gone to determine God's will for Stacey. She reas-sured me God knew Stacey's needs better than anyone else did. "He will make Stacey aware of His love and of yours."

"Joni, I feel like I'm losing it."

She gently replied, "God didn't require a brain to respond to us. He doesn't waste time. He certainly wouldn't waste two months."

The conversation ended as Joni prayed, "May the peace of the Lord be with you and keep your mind and heart in Christ Jesus."

Through Joni, God again expressed His desire to fill me with His peace and keep me sane.

—•—

Sunday morning, October 31:

I had no strength to make the trip to the hospital. I knew many relatives and friends from near and far had planned to spend some time with Stacey to say goodbye. Knowing she would not be alone, I stayed with my husband and our other children in the sheltering quiet of our home.

Dona, one of my closest friends, visited Stacey around 3:00 p.m., approximately twenty minutes before she died. Later, Dona described her last moments with Stacey:

Music played softly. Her breathing, far from effortless, had an ominous rattle. I held her hand and talked to her. I told her how much you loved her. 'Your mom loves you so much. She just wants so much for you not to suffer. Stacey, it's okay if God reaches His hand out to you, and you take it. Just take it. Your mom will be all right. We will take care of her.' I saw a little tear escape from Stacey's eye. Maybe it was just one of those things God does. I know what the doctors were all saying. I don't know. I prayed the Lord's Prayer with her, then left. The music played on. I remember sitting on the steps in the stairwell just outside her room. I wanted to go back in, but God's calmness said, 'No, just be still and know that I am God.'"

—•—

Around noon, I joined my brothers and sisters for lunch at my sister Bonny's home.

At the same moment Dona prayed releasing Stacey, I beseeched God to take her. Locked in my own world, unaware of others, weary and worn, my only memory, a brief unspoken plea: *God, You'd better take her soon. I'm beginning to doubt Your mercy.*

The longer I tarried, the more I knotted up. "I'm going to the hospital."

Joined by my brother Steven and his wife, Sandy, I trudged down the hospital corridor, planning to read the Scriptures with Stacey.

Approaching her room I said, "That's strange. Why is the door closed in the middle of the day?"

Someone stood waiting outside her room. "Stacey just died minutes ago." Reverently she opened the door for me.

I rushed to Stacey's side and wrapped her in my arms. "She's still warm." I held her for a moment then started to cry softly, "I'm so sorry, Stacey. So sorry."

I asked Steven to pray, but he choked up. Before he could get any words out, prayer graced my lips.

Earlier, the hospital had called Ronnie and told him Stacey died. He walked in just as I began to pray. Trembling, I whispered my prayer, bent over her, reaching, yearning to hold her warm body once again. I believe I began to sob. Ronnie gently pulled me away from her.

Steven, initially upset Ronnie wouldn't let me have a few more moments with her, later realized and told me, "Ronnie was protecting you. If he hadn't taken you away, I knew you probably would have held her forever."

———

November 3:

Leaden skies christened her burial. My shoulders shook as I wept at the graveside. God was not going to heal her—ever. She was gone. Her lifeless body lowered into the gaping, frozen ground. I wanted to look away. I couldn't. Tears gushed from a bottomless well. My legs lost all feeling. I began to fall. My heart also fell into a pit of despair. Powerless. I collapsed. Ronnie gathered me into his arms and led me to the car.

I had arranged for family and friends to join us after the funeral in Sneaky Hollow. This wooded niche had been a favorite gathering spot for Stacey and her friends. Because music had played an important part in Stacey's life, I asked musician Woody Wolfe to play his guitar. I'd hoped singing around the campfire would bring comfort.

Part of me didn't want those guests to go home that night, or ever. Nevertheless, one-by-one, they said their goodbyes; even those who traveled from great distances were gone the next day.

I felt more alone than ever.

———

Reason wrestled to make sense of something only God understood. Doubt tormented. *How could I have mistaken God's voice? He spoke through the shepherds, through the counselors, through the medical tests and the MRIs. Didn't He?*

A counselor tried to point me in the right direction, back to God and off my works to discern his will. "Don't let someone else cheapen the incredible lengths to which you went to determine God's will as best you could. You did the best a parent could do."

In November, Joni called. She too tried to turn my attention from my self-loathing back to God. "Wisdom," she said, "is trusting God." She quoted Hebrews:

> For God is not unjust to forget your work and love which you have shown to His name, in having ministered and in still ministering to the saints. And we desire that each one of you show the same diligence so as to realize the full assurance of hope until the end, that you do not be sluggish, but imitators of those who through faith and patience inherit the promises. (Hebrews 6:10–12)

"God is not unjust," Joni continued. "God was aware of all the effort you put forth out of love for your daughter and honor to God." She assured me He had intimate knowledge of my service in His name. He wouldn't forget my efforts, my prayers, or my sincere desire for Him to receive glory from this experience.

Pastor Schultz told me who had contacted Joni. It was Maria. The Sunday before Stacey died, I had asked her to pray for us as we made the horrific decisions. Joni wrote the letter, based on what Maria told her. A few weeks after Stacey's death, Maria called to see how we were doing. She began the conversation with small chitchat.

Infuriated by her nonchalance, I stopped her mid-sentence. "Did you contact Joni?"

"Yes."

"Do you have any idea how much harder that made it for us? A million times harder."

She had no idea the devastation wrought by her interference—repercussions reverberated throughout my entire family. Over the ensuing months, I grew more and more depressed as I carried around a huge load of guilt and unforgiveness.

Years later, in a discussion with Pastor Schultz, his comments about Maria helped me to sort through some of the logistics leading up to the letter:

> To me, it looked like it was so black and white to Maria with no extenuating circumstance or anything to dialog. I think right-to-life was just her main cause. I remember when she said she would personally be willing to take care of Stacey for the rest of her life.
>
> I was very concerned that you were caught in the middle between her and your husband. He made his decision to withdraw life support earlier than you. Since he was really not connected to the church and wasn't on the same wavelength with you as far as spiritual issues, I was very concerned her attitude could push him farther away from the Lord.
>
> As soon as she heard about Stacey, she became very proactive about it. I tried to encourage her to stay out of it. I just didn't feel it was something she needed to be involved in, and I told her so.

Nevertheless, believing she knew what God wanted, she contacted Joni. When Joni realized the scope of Stacey's initial injury, the resulting devastation to her brain, the extensive medical input and spiritual counsel I sought, she could then understand our decision to withdraw life support.

I can't rationalize why, even after Joni apologized and followed up with several phone calls, I still believed *I killed Stacey.* I see now those words did not come from Joni. They did not come from God, nor did they even ultimately come from Maria. The condemnation erupted from deep within me. My own self-condemning voice echoed Satan's, driving me to a pit of despair.

Perfectionism perpetuated guilt. David Gates' words came back to me: "Perfectionism is insidious. It is destructive of grace." Perfectionism led me headlong into a spirit of control. I needed to face these problems and take responsibility for my unresolved conflicts before I could begin to be free and recover from the loss of my daughter.

Coping Strategies

- Keep going: If your counselor or pastor isn't equipped to help you work through the trauma, seek out others. The Compassionate Friends support group exists to provide friendship, understanding, and hope to those who are grieving.

- Caution: Numbing the pain with overuse of drugs or alcohol will only complicate matters. Use medication only under the supervision of your doctor and only as directed.

CHAPTER 22

The Forks in the Road— My Crisis of Belief

*The word crisis comes from a Greek word that means
"decision." This crisis is not a disaster or a bad thing.
It is a turning point or a fork in the road that calls for a
decision. You must decide what you believe about God."*[36]

Henry Blackaby, Richard Blackaby and Claude King
from *Experiencing God*

Several times during this life-changing journey, I faced a fork in the road that called for a decision regarding what I believed about God. Three interrelated crises in my belief system troubled me: God's provision of Heaven, God's love for me, and God's sovereignty. The process of resolving those crises required hard work, honesty, and vulnerability. The journey was long and arduous. Would this experience confirm my belief in God or shatter it?

I believed God took Stacey to Heaven, and I knew God warned, "If you do not stand firm in your faith, you will not stand at all" (Isaiah 7:9, NIV). Nevertheless, guilt pummeled me. An image of her body, dead and frozen in the ground, tormented me. It broke open my wounded heart. I knew Stacey was not in that grave; yet, this impression of her decaying body robbed the joy of my vision of Stacey in Heaven with Jesus, clothed with a new beautiful body—one that would never decay.

My peace of mind vanished whenever I dwelled on the bleak side of death. Holding onto her while she was alive was far easier than letting go of her after she died. I couldn't walk away from her and live my life again. My guilt and sorrow over her death chained me to her. During those hellish days, I felt I might as well have buried myself with her.

My dear friend Kit helped me identify my problem so I could move beyond my doubts and fears. She said, "The Lord has told me fear has bound you to hurt and grief—fear that if you start releasing the hurt, the grief, and the guilt, you will somehow lose touch with Stacey and start to forget her. That's Satan's lie to make you afraid to lay down these burdens. If you lay them down, you'll start to remember the good times with Stacey, and the good memories will overcome and replace the bad memories you have now.

"God wants to bring you to the point of rejoicing with Stacey. She is now where there's no more death, mourning, crying, pain, hunger or thirst.

"Stacey has total joy in God's presence forever. There's a golden strand coming down from Heaven, connecting you with Stacey. She's now joined the cloud of witnesses that surrounds us" (Rev. 21:4; 7:15–17).

If I were ever to see that golden strand and feel any positive connection with God or with my daughter again, I needed to turn away from the horrific images so I could walk into the future with joy in my heart. After much soul-searching, I decided to face this obstacle and others head on. Kit and her husband Chuck prayed with me many times over the next months. They thought of an idea that helped me to see Stacey alive in eternity with God rather than dead in the grave. They asked me to imagine her upon an altar. I envisioned a large grey stone slab like the one on which they laid the crucified Savior.

Then they encouraged me to speak with my Lord out loud. I prayed for the words I needed to say. "Stacey is your child, God, not mine. Here she is. I give her back to You."

Next, I spoke to my daughter, "I love you, Stacey. Goodbye, darling." Then, in my mind's eye, I saw myself turn and walk away from the altar. I left Stacey with the Lord and released her totally to Him. I surrendered myself and my daughter to God. This turning point in my journey—the agony of walking away from her in this way—was vital to my recovery from the physical and emotional loss of her.

My second crisis of belief involved my perception of God's love for me. Did I believe God still wanted an intimate relationship with me, having allowed life support to be withdrawn from Stacey?

This crisis of belief resurfaced when the letter arrived and again after Stacey died. I believed this lie: I believed my weakness, my failure to discern God's will, could be greater than God's power to forgive. Haunting thoughts hounded me: *If my decision was contrary to God's will, could God ever forgive me? Could He forgive such a horrific blunder? Would He? Will He still love me? Or will He keep me at arm's length in some remote corner of Heaven? He might tolerate me, but He will never want the intimate relationship with me we once enjoyed.*

For some time after Stacey's passing, I didn't sense God's embrace or His presence, the comfort of His Spirit. Barrenness replaced our sweet fellowship. I couldn't receive His mercy and kindness. I felt unworthy, my self-condemnation justified. Intense spiritual loneliness threatened to drown me. The river from which this loneliness flowed raged endlessly, carrying me through deep waters of desperation. Life leaked out of me, draining from gaping heart holes.

My accusations against God heightened. *Why did You let me make the wrong decision? Why didn't You do more? How could You let me "kill" my daughter? Why didn't You stop me, God?*

Gradually, however, through Scriptures, meditation, and prayer, I began to understand I had relied on my behavior to win God's love, which fueled a legalistic attitude. I had believed that to be worthy of God's love, I had to adhere to His rules—with perfection. The tentacles of legalism entwined themselves around me; then the shackles of fear, control, perfectionism, and guilt squeezed out my joy. I lived by some of those destructive thought patterns for longer than I could remember. When Stacey died, all of my Christian "oughts" and "shoulds" cut through me. However, the mutilation did not come from Jesus. He teaches us to gently restore one another. I had condemned myself.

I now see that God used this horrific trial to show me my pride and my self-righteous attitude. Recognition of these tendencies revealed a two-fold arrogance. First, I strove to comprehend God, who is beyond my understanding. Second, through my actions, I strove to make myself more desirable to God.

At the time of Stacey's death, and even months after her passing, when God tenderly spoke with me, my unyielding and headstrong attitude continued to interfere with my freedom in Christ and strained my relationship with Him. In no way did I feel the closeness to God that I had thrived on in the past. I had not yet died to the tyranny of self.

Nevertheless, God held onto me, and, despite all my misgivings, I held onto Him with tenacious faith. Oswald Chambers said, "Tenacity is more than hanging on, which may be but the weakness of being too afraid to fall off. Tenacity is the supreme effort of a man refusing to believe that his hero is going to be conquered."[37] With stubborn faith, I persevered in my belief in who God is and what God says. I clung with white-knuckle faith to His gracious promise to bring good from this tragedy.

My third crisis of belief revolved around God's sovereignty. Who controlled my life, God or me? How could He bring good from this experience? When would He?

There's much wisdom in the saying, "Life must be lived forward but can only be understood backward." If I were ever to truly benefit from His promised blessing through the experience, I needed to search my soul even deeper. I needed to take an in-depth look at my past to see the ways God had acted according to His sovereignty and goodness throughout my life.

I wish the lessons I'd learned from past times of spiritual turmoil had better prepared me for the present trauma of Stacey's injury and death. Over my lifetime, I invested a great deal of time and energy trying to understand the Scriptures in the context of suffering. Yet, why does a loving God allow bad things to happen? I couldn't answer that question, and, worse yet, I couldn't explain God in this context. After searching the Scriptures and pleading for answers, I finally rested in what little spiritual insight my shadowed mind could understand of God's ways.

Ultimately, I returned to the lesson God taught me years earlier—to trust Him even when I don't understand Him. He is always faithful, always good, always kind, and always merciful. I believe this is God's nature, even when I don't see evidence of it in what He does or doesn't do.

In the aftermath of Stacey's death, I didn't struggle to understand why He allowed Stacey's accident and her death. Instead, I struggled to understand why He allowed her death to happen as it did, which forced end-of-life decisions upon us.

God possesses absolute power. I do not. Nevertheless, I obsessed over the thought I somehow wielded control over Stacey's life or death. Control is deceptive. Illusions of perfection and control blocked my awareness of God's absolute sovereignty.

In my disillusionment, I questioned God's part and mine in this experience. Did I really hold myself up so high that I placed my own opinion, or those of others, above *His* word? In the midst of the crisis, I believed He had expressed His will through counselors, friends, family, clergy, medical science, and professionals. Now I doubted.

Joni's letter continued to haunt me.

After Stacey died, I needed renewed faith to believe God had, indeed, heard my cries to Him, that he had led me to make a choice in agreement with His good plan for Stacey. I longed for a word from Him. At times, He did speak to me during quiet meditation. Yet, for many months, God's silence was deafening. He allowed His silence to drive me to complete dependence upon Him.

Where had He gone? In my despair, I continued to reach out for Him through the Scriptures. But oh, how devoid of life they now seemed. In the depths of my soul I pleaded, *Where is the "living" part of Your Word? God, why can't I hear Your voice?*

Although I wanted to stop leading Bible study, the women wouldn't let me quit. The social service club members wouldn't allow me to resign from my responsibilities. But, oh, how useless my service to Him felt. Did anything matter if I couldn't feel the presence and power of God in it?

Over the months preceding and following Stacey's death, I received many encouraging notes, complementing my strong faith. Ironically, while others marveled at my strength, I struggled to depend on God's strength, not mine. In reality, I felt weaker than ever.

One Sunday, I rushed out of church sobbing. I cried to a friend who followed me, "I don't know what to do or where to go to escape this grief and guilt. Where is God?" Then in the next instant, I apologized, "I'm sorry. I'm so sorry." I was concerned that my "excessive" show of emotion might upset others. Thoughts pummeled. *I need to be strong. If I fall apart, others will think God isn't taking care of me. I don't want to disappoint God.* This façade prevented me from moving beyond my loss.

When would I stop concerning myself with how I appeared to others? When would I stop saying, "I'm fine," when I wasn't? When would I realize how completely I had fallen into the traps of perfectionism, legalism, and control? When would I turn away from this false sense of security and value and turn to the grace, peace and rest of Christ?

Not for years.

God is sovereign in all circumstances. Throughout all of life's twists, turns, and forks in the road, He remains Sovereign God. I'm so thankful that throughout my journey, although questions sometimes plagued me, He never allowed me to lose my faith in His power, His purpose, or His sovereignty. My belief in the sovereign power of God and in His good intent remained the paradigm through which I viewed all of life.

Although Satan repeatedly tried to wrench this belief from me, I held to my faith with a vice-like grip throughout my journey. Yet, like a stubborn goat, I butted my head against His sovereignty many times over the next years.

Today I know I'm as dear to Him as ever. I find my relationship with Christ ever more intimate. He opens my eyes to see Him differently than I did before Stacey's death. Now I see He waits for me when I run to Him from the deep waters of my life. We share sweet fellowship.

This meeting of hearts, this new way of viewing myself as God's child, did not begin until I got to the end of myself. This enlightenment and freedom did not happen instantaneously; it spanned many years and demanded intensive soul-searching. Gradually, God spoke to me about several obstructions impeding the flow of His love and peace within me. One by one, I needed to release them. When I humbled myself under His merciful hand, He gave me grace to move forward in my journey.

Christ had cleared the path before me; I finally followed His leading. The forks in the road, the crises of belief I encountered on my journey, required faith and action. I came to believe with an even deeper understanding that without faith, I could never please God. Without action, I could not proceed on the path God laid out before me. Laying aside my pride, I asked God for more faith, faith so I could face the enemy within, faith to walk in new freedom with Him as my guide, and faith to see the golden strand that connects Stacey, me, and all of His children to Him.

Coping Strategies

- Don't give up: Loss often catapults us into a crisis of life and faith. Others have faced crisis, survived, and even grown stronger as a result of their loss. You can, too.

- Take one step at a time: Ask God to show you what steps He wants you to take so that you can continue your journey to recovery, complete the pain of your loss, and live a joy-filled life.

CHAPTER 23

Satan's Prison and God's Promise

I couldn't break free.

Over the winter months following Stacey's death, I started to acknowledge my guilt-ridden mindset, which was rooted in fear. God revealed to me the source of the guilt. It came from Satan himself. I often found myself returning to my prison of guilt where I walled myself in with bricks of legalism, perfectionism, control, and unforgiveness. God helped me see how I had laid each guilt-brick and applied the mortar of fear that cemented them together. He showed me how to knock each one down, one by one.

Until I faced their ugliness and released them, those attitudes held me hostage. I couldn't break free. I couldn't feel the steady and loving embrace of my Savior or experience joy.

In the spring, I saw the flowers reaching forth from the ground to the warm sky. This new birth seemed the antithesis of my daughter's death.

It shouldn't be this beautiful. These flowers shouldn't be here. Stacey is gone, buried beneath the same earthen floor that produces all of this beauty.

When thoughts of the future without my daughter produced a deluge of drowning tears, one particular prayer spurred me on in my journey. "Lord, daring to dream again sounds so good, but sometimes memories of broken dreams haunt me. Help me let go of the pain, which prevents me from responding to your gentle nudging. Your presence encourages me to set aside fear and to become a spiritual risk-taker. I want Your dreams for me to be my dreams as well. Amen."[38] God comforted me when I choked out that prayer.

My friend Lorraine penned a Scripture promise in large black letters on parchment, which I taped to the window over my kitchen sink. I recited it often with tears falling into the dirty dishwater draining down, down, until finally dispersing into hidden springs. My anguished heart bled sorrow until it seemed one with the earth, the same black earth that now held my daughter's shell.

I felt devoid of life—emptied out. Yet, this Scripture whispered reassurance. *Humble yourself. Cast all your cares upon Him.* I began to realize if I could follow these directions, one day God would lift me from my earthy grave. I looked up Lorraine's verse in different Bible translations and made a copy of the passage from the Amplified Bible. The instruction in 1 Peter chapter 5 became my lifeline. I copied verse ten on a thin slip of paper and carried it with me everywhere:

And after you have suffered a little while, the God of all grace [Who imparts all blessing and favor], Who has called you to His [own] eternal glory in Christ Jesus, will Himself complete and make you what you ought to be, establish and ground you securely, and strengthen, and settle you.

This promise wrenched me from the deepest pits of sorrow and grief. The apostle's words became my lifeline. The Lord's promise remained taped to the window over my sink for at least two years supplying a constant stream of hope. If I put myself in His hands, in His time, He would lift me out of my pit. His words urged me to cast my brokenness before Him, not to hide it under a false façade of strength and joy—but rather to be genuine with Him because He cared about me. He cared about our daughter. He reassured me that, after I had "suffered for a little while, the God of all grace, who called [me] to His eternal glory in Christ, [would] Himself perfect, confirm, strengthen, and establish [me]" (1 Peter 5:10).

I resolved to resist all pride in my works and surrender myself under His loving hand. Only then would I feel His strong arms around me. Only then could I receive His healing balm for my wounded spirit. Only then could I rest in His embrace.

God began to speak to me of a Sabbath rest. Scripture says rest is available to us after we have done all we can do, all God directs us to do. Then we *must* rest in Him. Otherwise, He cannot restore our strength and prepare us spiritually, emotionally, physically, and mentally for His next assignment. I began to realize my success depended on Sabbath rest. Another verse encouraged, "In repentance and rest is your salvation, in quietness and trust is your strength" (Isaiah 30:15, NIV).

He convinced me: "I must stop striving. I must rest in God. I will never be victorious in this trial unless I am still before God."

As a child runs to her father, I turned to the Lord of the Sabbath. Resting in Him gave me new strength and renewed my confidence in His promise to turn it all around for my good and His glory. Every time my mind turned away from the rest God offered, I needed to run back to Him, to the truth of who He is and what He says.

In reflection now, I'm deeply saddened that in the days immediately following Stacey's death, I didn't enjoy a lot of "rest." These words from Isaiah 30:15 depicted my experience more accurately: "But you would have none of it."

When I turned from His unfailing love and depended on my feeble efforts, I entered the darkest valley of my life. Desolation and depression washed over me like a flood. Before Stacey's accident, I felt close to God. At this point in my life, I felt utterly alone and hopeless.

Could it be what I desperately had hungered and thirsted for was God's unfailing love? Could this love be what I had searched for in countless people, places, and things? Nothing more—nothing less than God's love? I believe God Himself placed this craving within me—long before I was born. God called me to a relationship with Him. He placed emptiness within me only He could fill. Nothing else would satisfy my soul's longing.

Author Ann Voskamp quotes Francis de Sales who "gently, rightly urges, 'O my soul, thou art capable of enjoying God; woe to thee if thou art contented with anything less than God.'" Voskamp continues, "Does earth have anything I desire but Him? I have to ask it. And I know the answer: When I remember the gifts and how He loves me … I am moth drawn again to His ardent flame."[39]

God would one day use this darkest part of my life to draw me even closer to the flame of His love. He continued to call, but depression and self-punishing guilt deafened me to His voice. I couldn't find relief. I couldn't receive it. I felt unworthy of intimacy with God. Though I yearned and thirsted for His closeness, I had cut myself off from Him. Nothing brought satisfaction, not the council of pastors, Bible study, prayer, books, counselors, or work. No one. Nothing.

However, strength did come from God's Holy Word. Without the promises in Scripture, despair would have swallowed me in death. My mother provided day-by-day spiritual support, without which I couldn't have survived. She listened to biblically sound Christian leaders and shared her notes with me. She copied Scriptures and sent them to me, her Christ-likeness evident in so many ways. She helped around the house and cared for my children. Most importantly, she prayed continuously for me and with me, asking others to intercede on my behalf.

I continued to struggle as I worked through the pain and emotional turmoil. At first, I threw myself into many activities. I returned to college and began to write and speak of the experience, which helped me to understand intellectually what had happened to Stacey and verbalize my loss; yet, it did little to complete my recovery from it.

Counseling and self-help books could take me only so far. I felt even more a victim with no hope of a cure for my guilt, no way to pay off my debt to Christ, and no solution for my "sin." Bible study, prayer, and meditation helped to calm my anxiety, but they had not yet touched the source of my fear and loss.

Inside and outside of the home, I worked relentlessly, volunteering for long hours, immersing myself in service organizations and church activities. I worked inordinate hours outside in my yard, giving me a physical outlet for my pent-up emotional energy, yet nothing healed the source of my pain.

I began a pattern of leaving the house to begin my yard work at sunrise. I stayed outside until after dusk, only coming in to prepare lunch and dinner for the family.

One evening, my son Casey confronted me, gripping my shoulders. His angst-filled face echoed the pain in his voice. "Mom this isn't normal. Why do you do this every day? Please stop this. Come inside." Although I can't remember my immediate response, his words got through to me. I dropped the garden tools, but not the pain, and followed Him inside.

Along with my broken heart and crippling guilt, my marriage suffered. Anger, resentment, and bitterness toward my husband festered. He was so often absent. I felt no connection between us. Thus, all those forces exacerbated my quest for intimacy with God.

My prison walls closed in around me. I plummeted. I fell into a bottomless pit, where I gasped in rancid air—no shadows, no light. I hit bottom—the lowest point of my life.

By the spring of 1994, I had crawled down so far into my self-constructed prison, hope to ever again feel joy slipped beyond my grasp.

I had recently read the story in the Bible of God's prophet Elijah. At his lowest spiritual point, he literally ran in fear for his life. Discouraged and depressed, he felt abandoned although he had just experienced two great spiritual victories. Elijah found a dark, musty cave in which to hide. He "prayed that he might die," and said, "It is enough! Now, Lord, take my life, for I am no better than my fathers!" After God spectacularly displayed His power to Elijah through mountain-pulverizing wind, scorching fire, and tumultuous earthquake, He spoke to the prophet in a still, small voice: "What are you doing here, Elijah?" (1 Kings: 17–19).

On the morning of April 8, 1994, I expressed my own desire to God for relief through death. "Why am I alive and Stacey dead, Lord? Why didn't you take me instead?"

Through it all, God had followed me into my darkness. God came to my "cave" and spoke to me.

My journal entry contains the whole of His message, but the following portion of this revelation from God, a miraculous expression, became as oxygen to my gasping soul. In a whisper, God spoke to my heart:

> "What are you doing here, my child? Your daughter is with me. Why is your spirit so troubled?"

[I answered]

> "Where am I? I'm sitting in the muck and mire. I don't know if I am even trying to get out or if I care to get out. I deserve to be here. I have done a terrible thing, my Lord. I deserve to be in dust and ashes.
>
> "Where's my joy? I don't know. I don't know why it left. I don't know if I can get it back. Restore me, Lord.
>
> "I chose to end my daughter's life."

[God spoke to my heart]

> "But I chose before you, my child. She's with me.
> I chose before you.
> I chose before you started praying.
> I chose before the accident.
> I chose before she was born.
> I chose before she was conceived.
> You could have kept her body with you.
> But I had already chosen that Stacey would not have any active interaction with your world. I chose before you."

Finally, I understood. God had decided when Stacey's life would end. I never possessed the power. He had already decided.

He continued *"Begin to praise Me. There will be healing in that praise. I will lift you, direct Your way, and guide you out of this place."*

God's promise gave me the impetus and strength to move from the place of despair and to continue on my journey to recovery. He helped me to see how I had laid each guilt-brick that imprisoned me and how to knock each one down.

Coping Strategies

- Don't give in: to depression, self-defeating thoughts, or destructive actions. Go to your personal physician, counselor, pastor, or your community library or bookstore and ask what resources are available for one dealing with loss, grief, and guilt.

- Call or text trained counselors: They are available 24/7 to talk about anything that's on your mind.

- Keep hoping: Meditate on scriptural promises, prayers, uplifting literature, prose, or poetry from which you can derive hope.

CHAPTER 24

Mortar for my Prison Walls

Remember God in your past. Believe God in your present. This is the stuff of transformation.[40]

Beth Moore from *Believing God*

Through this experience, I've learned recovering from grief, like forgiveness, doesn't just take time; it takes work. It takes accepting responsibility for my feelings and my reactions to the events that have occurred throughout my life, thereby setting me on my present course. Accepting responsibility for my part in the situation and my reaction to it empowers me to change, at least, part of it. This truth facilitates freedom. If I ever were to recover from the loss of my daughter, I needed to retrace the steps in my life's path that programmed me to react to the loss as I did.

Throughout our lives we experience various losses: loss of relationship, health, career, finances, and numerous others. Recovery from loss is vital. Incomplete recovery can result in lifelong negative effects on the health, happiness, and wholeness of the individual. If we fall and suffer a gushing wound, we seek immediate medical attention to stop the bleeding and take steps to promote healing. We often neglect to attend to the needs of wounded hearts and strained beliefs. Incomplete recovery from physical, emotional, or spiritual crisis may cause loss of faith. Relationships with God and others sometimes suffer irreparable damage.

The authors of *The Grief Recovery Handbook* wrote:

> When we make other people or events 100 percent responsible for causing our feelings, then we also make them responsible for ending our feelings. … We have been falsely socialized to believe that we are victims of events and helpless in our responses to those events, as well as to the thoughts, feelings, and actions of others.[41]

For a long time after Stacey's death, I felt like a victim, already my posture toward my husband. In the wake of Stacey's death, I looked at Maria's involvement and attributed much blame to her for my deep depression and struggle with guilt and grief.

Those beliefs, among others, were lies I told myself and of which Satan took full advantage. As I worked through my grief and reflected on my life, God began to reveal the mortar paving my prison walls.

God used a Bible study, *Believing God*,[42] to show me how much power I had given to negative mindsets. The author, Beth Moore, encouraged readers to survey their lives for those times in which God had intervened. I searched the pages of my life for all the losses. I believed in God's enduring faithfulness, presence, and pursuit. Still, I needed Him to show me the ways He participated in *all* those experiences, even painful ones.

I wanted to recall His presence, His activity, all the times He had spoken to me, all the life lessons He had taught me. I asked God to reveal the ways in which He had worked to complete His plan for my life. I longed for Him to lead me into new revelations of His way and His will. I wanted to learn all He had to teach me so once again I could experience His abiding presence and the joy of His fellowship. Over time, I did see evidence of His patience, consistency, and grace.

One significant event I recalled from my distant past occurred at around the age of six or seven years when a teenager molested me. Thankfully, the Lord didn't allow the abuse to continue. Mother asked my oldest brother Drexel to watch over me to make sure the young man never again hurt me. I don't remember ever again discussing the incident at any length with my mother or anyone else. Perhaps, that's when I began to learn to grieve alone. I learned not to talk about problems. It also might have planted the seeds of my issues with control.

As a child and into my adulthood, my mother made the greatest impact on my Christian belief. She took everything to God in prayer. More than any other person, Mother taught me about the character of Christ. She taught me about having hope when all seemed hopeless. She taught me to trust God when nothing indicated a good outcome. She provided a wonderful example of constant love and forgiveness.

My father worked long hours. He often stopped at the neighborhood tavern after work. Although I suffered great loss through the absence of my father, mother's faithfulness and trust in God through all the years of Dad's drinking inspired faith and trust in me toward my Heavenly Father. Mother taught me about patience and enduring love as Dad continued drinking. She believed that one day God would answer her prayers. He did. Dad quit drinking around the time of the birth of my youngest sister Tammy.

Unfortunately, Mother didn't model confrontational skills, such as how to effectively communicate with others when upset or angry or how to resolve disagreements. I heard her call pastors and others to pray. I never heard her confront my father. To me, most often she suffered in silence, alone with God.

As an adolescent, I had given my heart to God. At twelve years old, my relationship with God became even more important to me when doctors diagnosed my father with nephritis. My oldest sister, Mary Ann, tackled many needs incurred by a large family, so Mother could concentrate on nursing Dad. Many times, as the next oldest daughter, the responsibility of my younger siblings fell to me when Mother and Mary Ann were absent. Finally, Mary Ann and her husband found us a home in Rhode Island near a veterans' hospital where my father could receive kidney dialysis.

Ultimately, my father suffered a long, painful death from kidney disease. Mother modeled unswerving love and faithful service. Nevertheless, I had no power over my father's illness or the losses associated with it, which most likely reinforced my issues with control. Although the experience taught me to buck up, take responsibility, and be strong, it likewise left me very little time to enjoy my adolescence. I never grieved the loss of my childhood.

As a teen, I looked to others and to my own accomplishments rather than to God for my sense of value. I turned away from what I knew to be God's will for me. I knew God had set a standard to live by and guidelines to protect me and to honor Him. Reared in the church, I knew the basics of God's good plan for my life. Although philosophical and contemplative by nature, I still didn't understand God had set His behavioral boundaries for my protection because He loved me. I needed to obey and not manipulate His truth to justify my actions.

Around the time of my father's illness, I met Ronnie. My relationship with God suffered when I tried to please Ronnie rather than obey God. I tossed back and forth like a rowboat caught in a tempest. I looked to a man to fulfill my need for intimacy and significance rather than looking to God. Perhaps I turned to Ronnie because of some lack in my relationship with my father. Nevertheless, I denied God's Lordship over my body, my thoughts, and my actions.

My teenage years were in complete turmoil, beginning with Dad's illness. In many ways, my adolescence ended when my father became ill and I met Ronnie. Nothing seemed carefree from that time forward. I looked to Ronnie to meet needs God never intended him to satisfy. I continued to believe in God, although I walked in disobedience to His will for me. I still prayed to Him, read my Bible, and went to church. In retrospect, I discovered God is faithful even to His rebellious children. God honored my mother's prayers and kept all of us children safe.

Sadly, I entered my marriage ill-equipped. Instead of confronting my husband and discussing problems when they surfaced, I prayed, and I asked others to pray. I didn't effectively communicate my feelings to him. This gulf in our relationship deepened. When Stacey died, I shared very little of any of my painful issues surrounding her death. When I tried to communicate my feelings to him, I felt misunderstood. Often, I suffered in silence.

About four years after Ronnie and I married, I had a miscarriage, a loss I had not yet dealt with at the time of Stacey's accident. Having never worked through the loss of the child, I transferred the negative energy generated from the experience into anger and frustration toward the doctors and, perhaps, even toward my dear husband.

As I grew older, disappointment filled me even more when Ronnie did not—or could not—meet my needs for emotional intimacy and significance. With no spiritual connection, we grew more and more distant from one another. I doubted my husband's love for me. The seeds of resentment and bitterness toward my husband thrust their roots even deeper. I depended more heavily upon family, friends, and church to supply my needs.

I had empowered my husband to affect how I felt about myself. I dwelled on the words he spoke to me, or of me, rather than the truth of what God speaks to me and about me. I placed his opinion of me, or my perception of it, above who God says I am. I allowed my husband's affection, his attention, and his approval to have more impact on me than the affirmations of God. I tied my joy too closely to my husband.

I also doubted God's love for me. I believed I needed to do everything right, to understand everything in order to please God and win, or somehow be worthy of, His love. The seeds of this lie germinated in me as a young child and continued to grow into my adulthood.

When I buried myself in guilt after Stacey's death, it hit me hard. I listened to someone else's voice other than God's. First, my own self-condemning voice, next Joni's voice, finally the voices of countless imagined others whom I feared judged me for the ways I believed I failed in my actions or attitude. I robbed myself of my worth and allowed my own opinion or that of another to determine my identity and value.

At the time of Stacey's death, unaware of these destructive tendencies, I couldn't get beyond the pain of my loss of her or connect emotionally to my husband until I broke free from their negative influence. There's great wisdom in the saying, "You are free when you loosen your grip on something you were never meant to bear."[43] In the spring following Stacey's death, God asked me, "What are you doing here, child?" I had encased myself in chains of guilt. At that moment, I loosened my grip on guilt, and my heart began to mend. But I was not yet free.

In addition to clinging to Stacey, I also clung to other people and controlled various areas of my life with a vice-like grip. Over the years, I grew to depend a great deal on my mother, brothers, and sisters, which became strikingly evident when Stacey's accident happened. I appreciated their spiritual insight along with their comfort and support.

Now God showed me how I ran to my family instead of running to Him—especially when I didn't want to face the lessons He tried to teach me. My extended family often provided a short-term cure for my need to escape the pain of my loneliness and emptiness.

However, unresolved anger and resentment still simmered within. My attitudes and actions harmed others and dishonored the image of Christ in me. Meanwhile, the unresolved pain of earlier traumas continued to influence my reaction to crisis.

When would I confess my wrongs before God and say I was sorry? When would I ask for His forgiveness for assuming the false identities of pride, perfectionism, and guilt? When would I finally begin to walk in my identity as God's beloved child?

Although these obstacles were hard to face, the new awareness of them empowered me and gave me hope that one day God would help me overcome them. Only God could tear down the mortar of my prison walls and free me to respond in a healthy way to my present reality.

In order to recover and become emotionally and spiritually healthy, I needed to change my thinking—to allow God to change my view of Him, others, and myself. Then I could live life to its fullest. The Lord had much more for me. Over the next months and years, I fervently prayed, studied, and meditated. I asked God to open my heart to receive His love.

Several seasons passed before I faced the losses I experienced over my lifetime. In the midst of sorrow, I started to praise God. Praise opened the floodgate and released His love from deep within. As I began to sing or speak God's praise and thank Him—even for this dark valley—His love and forgiveness welled up from the depths of my soul. Praise brought sweet release.

The long-needed remedy for my broken heart arrived. God sent his only Son, Jesus Christ, to rescue me, to give His life for mine. Jesus took any punishment I deserved on Himself. Before Stacey's accident, I knew this truth in my mind. Could I hold it in my heart? I realized I didn't have to stay imprisoned or banished from God. He wanted to be closer than any spouse, relative, friend, or counselor could ever be. God wanted intimate knowledge of my thoughts and feelings. My Heavenly Father had made His home in me. He had even greater joy and freedom—all available in Christ—stronger love than I ever imagined.

The mortar of my prison walls began to crumble. God exposed two remaining obstacles to recovery: unforgiveness and a false self-identity. One day I would see a fuller revelation of His love for me, one that would unlock my prison doors, so I could fly from my shackles straight into His arms. One day He would produce a transformation in me as a butterfly escaping from its cocoon.

Long before Stacey's accident, when I first accepted Him as Savior, He came to live within me. He never left. He didn't just walk beside me through Stacey's death. He did more than carry me through it. He lived it with me and gave me the desire and power to overcome it.

I continued on my journey to freedom and joy in Christ.

Coping Strategies

- Be receptive: God will show you how much He loves you through the comfort and support of others.

- Take responsibility for your feelings and actions: You cannot control what happens to you, but you can choose your reaction to it. You do not need to continue reliving the pain of your loss and feeling victimized by the trauma. Seek out a grief recovery counselor.

- Praise God: When you praise God in the midst of the crisis, you will begin to heal. Listen to and sing praise and worship music. Don't isolate yourself from others or the world around you. Go out. Enjoy nature's praise song: singing birds, rustling leaves, and babbling water.

CHAPTER 25

Walking toward Forgiveness

*Life in Christ offers a perpetual opportunity
to begin anew.*

(2 Corinthians 5:17)

I became a new person when I invited Christ to live in my heart. However, I realized that each day I must consciously choose to trust Him and to follow His prompting.

Unfortunately, even years after accepting Christ as my Savior, I hadn't completely entrusted my life to Him. At the time of Stacey's accident, I didn't fully understand my relationship with God. I had not assumed my role as His child or assimilated the benefits that relationship afforded. For years, I walked among the living but felt like I was bleeding to death. I condemned myself. I played all the parts: judge, prosecutor, and executioner. I tried to nail myself on a cross, but I just couldn't pound in that last nail.

In reality, I could not crucify myself. The Reverend Nigel Mumford says of such attempts: "There will always be one more nail left."[44] There would always be one more blow needed to drive in the last nail of my self-inflicted torture.

Perfectionism germinates as a subtle addiction then grows into a destructive idol. My need to be good enough left me dissatisfied. In fact, religious activities stood between God and me. I devoted more energy and time to church work and Bible study than to my relationship with God. When I searched for a sense of significance apart from my identity in Christ, I became insecure, punishing, and driven. If I failed, I feared rejection—from others—and worst of all, from God.

I needed to reprioritize my time and my life and make my time alone with God the most important part of my day. During these quiet moments, He showed me another key to recovery. I needed to forgive others as God forgives them, in the same way He forgives me. That key would open my heart to receive more of His love. Then I could love others as He loved them. What God has forgiven, I have no right to hold on to.

Author Robert Jeffress says we emotionally bind ourselves to others who offend us when we refuse to forgive them. Thus, they have the power to inflict the same hurt repeatedly while we continue to relive the experience, and we take on a victim mentality. When we release others of the obligation to treat us as we feel we "deserve," we no longer relive the pain of the past. Remembrances of times when others have disrespected us no longer control our emotions, responses, or actions.[45]

My unforgiving spirit bound me to the very things I disliked in others. I prayerfully considered Mark 11:25: "Forgive, if you have anything against anyone, so that your Father who is in Heaven will also forgive you your transgressions." I remembered the verse Pastor Hoffman had shared with me from Matthew 16:19: " … whatever you bind on earth shall have been bound in Heaven, and whatever you loose on earth shall have been loosed in Heaven."

If I could genuinely forgive, I could release others from those bonds. God could then begin to work in my life and theirs to transform us into what He created us to be. I began to understand the change wouldn't happen because of my efforts but because of the work of the Holy Spirit in me. The change wasn't narrowed by my own agenda but was, and is, broadened to fulfill God's plan and purpose for each of us.

Forgiveness for anyone is not always automatic or easy. It's certainly not instinctive.

In the past, I had extended forgiveness to others. Nevertheless, I lacked closure. Sometimes I sought restoration of relationship, but the grief and pain surrounding those losses continued and deeply affected my personality. If I could have released and forgiven others as God forgives, I would've no longer perceived myself as a victim.

God showed me my need to extend forgiveness and love to several individuals. First and foremost, I needed to forgive God. Initially, I didn't think I blamed God, yet my journal entries expressed anger, confusion, and hurt as I raised pointed questions to Him. It took many years to be honest with myself and God and to admit my anger toward Him.

Asking for and receiving forgiveness from God are lifetime processes, each absolutely necessary in order to move ahead rather than remaining stuck like a needle caught in a scratch on a record. Unfortunately, I did keep going back. My questions replayed in my mind and heart.

Gradually, I understood the lesson God wanted me to learn didn't pertain to end-of-life decisions. Rather, God cared more about how I handled and responded to the crisis. I responded with an attitude driven by perfectionism and a controlling nature. I wish I had allowed the Holy Spirit to control me, so I could have reacted with grace and humility. I had little grace for my husband or for me, which I knew grieved God. Because He had saved me by His grace, I needed to extend His grace to others, especially to my husband.

God patiently waited as I continued to carry the baggage of unresolved pain and crippling unforgiveness. Sometimes He spoke to my heart, not audibly but to my soul. Asking Him to change my attitude and actions, my journal entries record His answers to my prayers.

November 8, 1994:

[*The Lord speaking to my heart*]

When you forgive Ronnie, you forgive me.
Will you forgive Ronnie for not 'being there' for you? Will you forgive Me? When you forgive him, you forgive Me.

Can you love Me without ever knowing why Stacey died as she did? You did not cause her death, my child. She was dying. I was allowing that to happen. I could have wakened her at any moment, even to the last breath. I could have given you another sign, some other way to go.

[*I respond*]

But you didn't God.

[*God speaks*]

Can you love Me even so? I've allowed this to happen to you and your daughter. Can you love Me now?

November 17· 1994:

[*Stacey speaking to my heart*]

He will still love you, Mom. Dad will still love you.

[*My spirit responding*]

Show me the way, Lord. Lead me through this valley of change.

Guide me, O thou great Jehovah, my Protector, my Provider, my Strength, my Peace, my Love, my All.

Keep my mind in perfect peace, O Lord. Keep my mind stayed on You.

My Father, my Lord, my King. I love You, with all my heart.

Help me, Lord, to love You more than I do at this moment.

Increase my love toward You. Restore my joy.

You are my Joy.

Be very real to me this moment, this hour, this lifetime.
I love You, Lord.

I forgave God when He entreated me in this gentle way. I began to forgive myself when God said, "You did not cause her death, my child."

Could I forgive Ronnie?

———————

I didn't realize I held my husband responsible for my joy—or the lack of it. With my victim mentality toward him, I took every rejection, perceived or real, to heart and allowed it to wound my spirit. My perception of how I should have been treated, my sense of rightness, or self-righteousness, restricted my life in many ways.

My perfectionist ideals, desires, and demands dictated how I evaluated our relationship on every level. My obsession with perfection and my failure to achieve it kept me from appreciating even the times my husband lovingly tried to provide for my needs.

I longed for emotional intimacy with Ronnie. Our communication as husband and wife had always been lacking. The trauma of Stacey's accident only accentuated that weakness. I wanted us to enjoy one another and share each other's interests. Those times seemed rare. In reality, we did share many special times as a family, but Ronnie spent so much time away from home, and even when he was there, I felt little connection between us. I resented him because, in my mind, he didn't even care about these things.

I narrowly focused on my husband's "failures" to meet my perceived needs—his absences and the hurts I experienced throughout our marriage. If my husband failed to live up to my high expectations, I sometimes unconsciously used unforgiveness toward him as a means of punishment. With the awareness of my narrow focus came a realization of how deeply my negative attitude affected my personality, my marriage, and other relationships. Concerning my husband, he often didn't deserve what I held against him. I needed to accept that I was responsible for my part in our troubled relationship.

At the time of Stacey's death, I felt Ronnie had not fully participated in the steps leading up to the decision for withdrawal of life support. I thought Ronnie made up his mind too quickly and had accepted the medical evaluations without enough input or secondary opinions.

I met with the doctors during the daytime hours while Ronnie worked. Naturally, I heard all the reports. I requested any added medical evaluations and sought extensive spiritual counsel. It was *my choice* to carry the responsibility of the decision. I chose to bear it, yet it grieved me that we couldn't make this decision regarding our daughter together.

Because my husband did not share my faith, he was not able to be there in the way I wanted him to be. Although my husband's struggles were not of a spiritual nature, as were mine, he suffered greatly as well. Not until years after her death did Ronnie share a few of the details of his involvement with Stacey's day-to-day care and of the extreme pressure he simultaneously experienced at work. During those dark days, not only did he endure stress from his daughter's imminent demise, but he also carried a heavy load related to his job.

Learning of his pain helped me to see things from his perspective and forgive him. I appreciated all the effort he invested in the decisions we made and into our relationship in the aftermath. I needed to respect the way my husband approached this trauma. Even though Ronnie did not choose to continue life support, he allowed me the time to come to the decision on my own. He showed me more respect and patience than I showed him. What did my indecision do to my husband? What torment did I inflict on him while I deliberated?

I believe Ronnie understood, long before I did, the ability to give Stacey life didn't lie within the power of either of us. The ventilator had not given her life; it only forced air into her lungs. While wrestling with these complex issues, one of my counselors said, "We're not going to strap God's hands no matter what decision we make." In my head, I agreed with the Psalmist, who declared, "Our times are in His hands" (Psalm 31:14–15, KJV). Somehow, my heart lost sight of that. I just couldn't let go.

Now I see we didn't in any way limit God's power when we removed life support. To a large degree, my unrealistic expectations blinded me to my husband's concern for Stacey and for me. It hindered me from benefitting from God's comfort and from my husband's attempts to console me.

Instead of concentrating on Ronnie's "flaws," I could have—should have—looked for the good things in his character that, to my chagrin, God's still showing me. Many qualities I perceived to be flaws in my husband were simply differences in the way men and women perceive reality, the way we deal with life.

My husband grieved differently from me. He spent a lot of time away from home, fishing and hunting. It took me years to accept that's just who he is. He intended me no harm. Nonetheless, alone, I felt abandoned. I'm sure I wasn't good company even when Ronnie came home. Guilt tormented both my conscious and subconscious thoughts. Many nights I tossed and turned. Rest rarely came.

I confess with deep regret the harsh and unkind judgment I inflicted on my husband. I judged his actions, his motives, even his spirituality.

God alone has the right to judge.

However, when I began to praise God, even in the midst of my sorrow, His presence in me and His influence over me grew stronger. I began to embrace what the Psalmist declares: "But thou art holy, O thou that inhabits the praises of Israel" (Psalm 22:3, KJV). I discovered forgiveness requires love, and in time, the Holy Spirit empowered me to forgive my husband and to begin to learn to love Ronnie as God loves him.

———

Besides showing me I needed to forgive Ronnie, God also brought to my attention my need to forgive Stacey and Marcus. I didn't even realize I harbored unforgiveness toward either of them, although biting regret for the circumstances surrounding the accident lurked deep inside my mind.

According to the police report, Marcus drove the car dangerously fast. I excused his irresponsibility because sometimes I know I do the same. I felt it was just an accident, after all. Yet, he had been the driver. I needed to accept the fact that his reckless behavior resulted in Stacey's death.

Harder to accept: I needed to forgive Stacey. If anger or unforgiveness existed, I didn't know it. I only wanted to take care of my daughter, to love her. Nevertheless, the accident had happened because Stacey made the decision to stay behind when we wanted her to come with us. She stepped out of character, called off work, and decided to go with Marcus that day even though she knew we expected her to stay close to home while we were away.

Despite circumstances which I felt had been avoidable, in time I did manage to extend my grace and forgiveness to Stacey and Marcus. Moreover, in time, I came to realize God had extended His mercy, not only to me, but also toward everyone involved.

Within a few short weeks after Stacey's death, I knew I must forgive Maria, who had contacted Joni. However, years passed before I completed the work of forgiveness toward her. My journal entries often reflected God's prompting to continue this walk toward forgiveness:

[*God speaking*]

"I am Who I am. I choose to be what I choose to be. I do love you. I did not mean it for your harm. You will be stronger because of this. I will not leave you alone. I will not forsake you here. I will see you through this. You will have more understanding of others. Your faith will be stronger.

I chose it to be as I chose it to be. I am your God. Rest in Me. With Me, you will be stronger. Lean on Me. Lean on others. Forgive her. It will make you stronger—what happened between you two.

I love you."

God's words comforted me and reassured me of my Father's love. They gave me hope to continue and not give up in my journey to recovery. They gave me courage to be honest with God, to tell Him everything and even confess my greatest failures. When I did, He never hurt me. He helped me. He helped me to be more like Christ, to think and act more like Christ.

The burden of anger and unforgiveness toward Maria wearied me. Not long after Stacey's passing, I went to Pastor Sommers, hoping he could help me deal with my unresolved feelings. When we prayed, I offered my broken heart to the Lord and asked Him to give me forgiveness toward her. Pastor Sommers suggested I write out a statement of forgiveness. The statement resembled a bank deposit slip. On a sheet of paper about the size of an envelope he wrote:

Pay to the order of _____ Maria

$ _____ Forgiveness

BANK OF GOD'S GRACE

Signature: _____

I signed and dated the forgiveness document. I knew I made a genuine commitment that day to forgive Maria. God honored that action. It was a start, but I couldn't just forgive her and move on because I still couldn't forgive myself.

For years, I attributed much of the pain and guilt I experienced after Stacey's death to Maria's involvement. I thought if she hadn't called Joni, who then wrote the letter, I wouldn't have taken on the paralyzing self-condemnation. I experienced intense emotional pain and suffering whenever I thought of Maria's unsolicited involvement and the unsettling letter that followed.

In Matthew 7:1–5, Jesus teaches about judging others:

Do not judge, or you too will be judged. For in the same way you judge others, you will be judged, and with the measure you use, it will be measured to you. Why do you look at the

speck of sawdust in your brother's eye and pay no attention to
the plank in your own eye? ... First take the plank out of your
own eye. (NIV)

Jesus' words directed me to deal decisively with any obvious sin
in my own life before I judged Maria. When she interfered, I felt
betrayed. Yet, I lacked objectivity. I couldn't put aside my personal
feelings and confront her. Ultimately, it took far less time and effort
to begin to forgive her than to forgive myself.

In time, I realized that Maria, like me, was motivated by what she
perceived to be God's will. He read both our minds, saw what lay in
our hearts, and allowed this experience to unfold as it did. All the
while, He remained sovereign over all, including Stacey's life.

Many years passed before I discussed these circumstances with
Maria again. She only vaguely remembered our last brief conversation. Shortly after Stacey's death, I had told her she made our tragedy even worse by contacting Joni. At that time, it seemed she had
made light of her involvement, and I sensed little remorse on her
part. However, years later when I reached out to her, she apologized
and expressed her sadness for the pain she had caused.

I accepted her apology without excusing her actions or making
slight of her interference in our affairs. Before ending the conversation, we both prayed. She prayed for my husband and me and asked
God to forgive her for her insensitivity at such a painful time.

At last, I felt great release.

Several years after Stacey died, I attended a small grief recovery
group, where I learned of the book, *The Grief Recovery Handbook*,
that recommends writing a pattern letter to various people.[46] The
exercise helped me to complete the pain of the losses I experienced
over my lifetime. It also provided the impetus to continue the work
of forgiving, necessary in order to move on with my life. The letters
I eventually wrote became more than a mere recitation of events and

rehashed emotions. They empowered me to say goodbye to what was incomplete or left unsaid in relationships.

When writing the letters, I found I could treasure fond memories of ways in which those relationships had enriched my life while also acknowledging specific unmet hopes and dreams surrounding the relationships. I said farewell to my list of unrealistic expectations of others who could not or would not meet those expectations. The letters didn't mean the end of a relationship, rather the expression of the ways in which the hurts influenced the relationship.

After writing my goodbye letters, I took the final step in the process. I read the letters aloud to one of my trusted grief recovery partners, one who attended the sessions with me under the direction of a certified grief recovery counselor. I wrote letters to my mother, my father, Stacey, Ronnie, and others. I did not anticipate the intense emotional reaction I would experience when I read the letter aloud to another living person. Pausing for tears, often with guttural resolve to say goodbye to these losses, I pressed the heavy words up and out from the depths of my heart. Remarkably, at the conclusion, I felt a sense of closure and an enduring peace, unlike the fleeting peace of my past.

———

During those dark years following Stacey's death, I located Scriptures that proved the truth about my relationship with Christ. I realized there were times I grieved God and times I failed to be honest and truthful with God, with myself, and with my husband. However, as I worked through my guilt, I latched onto the truth that even when I caused God sorrow, His affection toward me never waned. "God saved you through faith as an act of kindness. You had nothing to do with it. Being saved is a gift from God. It's not the result of anything you've done, so no one can brag about it" (Ephesians 2:8–9).

As I meditated on the Scriptures, I began to see how I had tied my value to my actions even before Stacey's accident. In many instances, I had perceived my value to be contingent upon my actions.

In Robert S. McGee's book, *The Search for Significance,* the author makes a profound statement, which changed my attitude toward others and myself: "I have great worth apart from my performance because Christ gave His life for me and therefore, imparted great value to me. I am deeply loved, fully pleasing, totally forgiven, accepted, and complete in Christ."[47]

Now I use this statement as a gauge for my life, to determine if I am walking in the light of God's truth about me or in a distorted image of the person He created me to be. I finally accepted that once I gave my life to God, Christ's own work, not my work, became the source of my value.

McGee speaks pointedly of our position and value as part of God's family, made possible by Christ's work at Calvary:

> You are acceptable to God! He does not just tolerate you. You are 100 percent acceptable to the highest Judge: the perfect, holy, and righteous God Almighty. You are accepted by God for one reason: Christ has abolished the barrier and made peace with God through His blood on the cross. You have the righteousness of Christ (2 Cor. 5:21). You can't ever be any more acceptable to God than you are now" (Rom. 5:8–10. Eph. 2:14–18. Col.1:21–22).[48]

So impressed by Magee's words, I copied this last poignant statement and others from the book, laminated them, and carried them and the Scriptures with me on my walks. In time, I realized only God has the right to condemn or save anyone. In arrogance, I had put myself in God's place of authority. God knows our hearts, understands our motives, and still loves us.

Because Jesus Christ took the punishment for our sins, when we declare our faith in Christ, God accepts us just as we are. God declared me "Not guilty." What a marvelous truth. As I grew in my understanding of who I was as a believer in God, I gradually discovered I didn't need to keep myself locked in a cage of punishing guilt. God's own Son, Jesus Christ had unlocked the door.

When I realized how intimately God loves me, how completely He forgives me, and how unconditionally He accepts me, I needed to take one more action.

I forgave myself. I followed Him out of the Valley of Unforgiveness.

After dark months and years, I released my husband and others from the burden of my unforgiveness. A new day was dawning. Still, God had not finished with me. He lifted me up when I became weary and weak. He made the path straight when I became disoriented and confused. Sometimes I waited for Him with patient endurance. Sometimes I impetuously ran ahead. Sometimes I stubbornly lagged behind. Yet, I persevered in my faith in God and in His power to transform me into the person He created me to be and to transform this tragedy into triumph.

Now I needed to step out into a new life with Him.

Coping Strategies

- Forgive others and yourself: Forgiveness frees you from a victim mentality and unlocks your heart to receive God's love and forgiveness.

- Write letters of forgiveness according to the pattern outlined in *The Grief Recovery Handbook*.

- Be open: Ask God to convince you of His acceptance, love, and forgiveness as you follow the steps outlined in Robert S. McGee's book, *The Search for Significance*.

CHAPTER 26

Finding Myself along the Way

Fear is the enemy of everything God wants to bring forth from your life. Fear will stop a [person] dead in [his] tracks and keep [him] there for years—even decades.[49]

Angela Thomas from *Do You Think I'm Beautiful?*

M y deeper understanding of God's forgiveness and His desire to be close to me led me down a new path. I craved a deeper knowledge of His love. As I hungered for God as never before, He helped me face obstacles that had hindered me from fully realizing His love.

My compulsion to please everyone, to follow all the rules, and do everything "right" acted as a cataract, clouding my vision of His love. I studied God's Word and poured all my energy and intellect into trying to understand it and apply His truths. That left little energy or time just to sit in His presence and allow Him to speak to my spirit. I was convinced of His truth in my mind but not in my heart. I had not given Him the opportunity to meet with me in stillness and quietness so He could commune with me. I lived in the emptied-out places of my life rather than in the Christ-filled abundance He desired for me.

God showed me how fear that I would disappoint Him stood as a barrier between us. At first, I thought the guilt I carried for "killing" my daughter separated us. The real barrier originated in my self-righteous attitude, which then bred fear, guilt, and anxiety.

As I became aware of my harmful attitude and behaviors, I saw my need to abandon my old ways of thinking and turn from the lies I told myself. Through prayer, Scripture, and counsel, I realized my self-destructive tendencies had become false identities. They didn't align with God's image in me.

From the beginning, God created humankind in His image (Genesis 1:26). God intended that He would receive glory as mankind reflected His nature and His attributes—all that was beautiful and perfect about Him.

When I invited the Lord into my life, He gave the gift of His Holy Spirit to re-create in me His very nature. I am God's child. That's my true identity. However, I didn't accurately reflect His image or His glory. I simply couldn't until I relinquished my false identities—only possible if and when I allowed the transforming power of the Holy Spirit to control and act through me (Acts 1:8).

God chooses His children and empowers them by Christ to bear His image of love, joy, peace, patience, kindness, goodness, faithfulness, gentleness, and self-control (Galatians 5:22–25). The beauty of His glory, His nature, doesn't automatically shine forth until we respond to the promptings of His Holy Spirit and ask Him to exchange our nature for His. Sadly, I often denied the Spirit's promptings and thus, dishonored and grieved God.

I allowed several pervasive false identities to take root within me. I exchanged God's image in me for something of far lesser value. On one hand, I believed my very breath came from God. Yet, I denied His image in me when I exchanged it for something of my own making, something like fear, pride, selfishness, bitterness, guilt, or perfectionism. I began to realize how stubbornly I clung to my right to indulge in these harmful characteristics.

I believe Jesus Christ grieves when we don't yield our nature to the Holy Spirit. He knows firsthand both the abounding joy found in obedience and the consequential pain resulting from separation by sin. He took our sins upon Himself and bore them in our place, so we could enjoy fellowship with God. Unfortunately, I hadn't taken full advantage of the gift of His sacrifice. My salvation in Christ was real, but my experience of it was not fully realized. I didn't live in the freedom of Christ (John 8:36).

As I read the Scriptures, prayed, and sought counsel, I began to ask God to change my thought patterns and replace them with His thoughts. As I approached God in this way, I saw my own attempts at perfectionism were meaningless when compared to the perfect life Jesus demonstrated. My feeble attempts either filled me with pride or wore me out as I struggled to attain that which Christ had already given to me.

Thankfully, over the months and years after we said goodbye to Stacey, God didn't allow me to despair to the point of death. Thoughts of her passing no longer consumed me. Yet, at times her death continued to press down upon me. Little by little, He encouraged and strengthened me as I worked through those issues.

In the fall of 2006, I left my job. Once again, I worked through my grief and the experience of Stacey's passing. A journal entry tells how the Lord continued to lead me through this journey:

[*I speak to God*]

"You came, Lord, and you spoke clearly to me: 'There was nothing for which you needed forgiveness, my child.'
Why then do I continue to struggle with this guilt?"

[*God answers*]

"Satan uses this to buffet you about with his fiery darts.
'Put on the whole armor of God that you may be able to withstand the attack and having done all, to stand' (Ephesians 6:13).
I love you my child."

In the midst of this turmoil, God wanted to protect me from the piercing arrows of the evil one, but I had left my shield down. Instead of putting on God's armor and resisting these negative behaviors, I had given them a foothold. Enlightened by what God spoke to me, I turned to Ephesians 6:10–18, which became my new defense against my false identities and helped me to walk in my true identity as a child of God. I copied those eight verses and made a conscious choice to begin each day meditating on them, asking for God's protective armor, his guidance, and discernment.

God brought to light several negative identities I had unknowingly accepted: guilt, anger, bitterness, and others. Those false self-images defined me. They became the gods controlling me, standing in defiance and opposition to God's intended purpose for my life. I had allowed these negative influences to accumulate in my soul, rather than holding up my "shield of faith" to deflect the "fiery darts" and keep them out (Ephesians 6:16).

Gradually, I accepted my responsibility for acquiescing to these mindsets. [50] I first acknowledged the false guilt I had taken on regarding Stacey's death. I believed the lie thundering in my soul: "You've killed your daughter! No one will love you when they find out."

The apostle Paul says " … there is now no condemnation for those who are in Christ Jesus" (Romans 8:1, NKJT). No condemnation!

Satan condemns. The Holy Spirit convicts. The outcomes are in direct opposition. In John 10:10 Jesus says Satan's intent is to "kill, steal, and destroy." Satan, the personification of evil, tried to kill my faith, steal my joy, and destroy my relationship with God and others.

The Holy Spirit shows us our guilt (convicts us of our sin), not to hurt us, but to teach, guide, and correct, drawing us closer to God and refining us to the image of Christ. Thankfully, God's power surpasses the power of evil (1 John 4:4). God's grace drew me closer to Him.

The Holy Spirit reminded me that as long as I admitted my failures to Him and asked for forgiveness, He'd not only forgive me for taking on a guilt-identity, He would also remove everything distancing me from Him.

God brought each of my false identities to my attention. He wanted to free me from them. God showed me how pride fueled my false identities. My heart, when filled with pride, had no room for God.

When I tried to earn my own salvation through my works, no room remained in my life for Christ's sacrifice. I had no room for passion when I wrapped my life in performance.

I learned pride repels the Lord. Contrition and humility draw Him. If I come to Christ with anything other than humility, I may as well not come at all. In order to be free of the things separating me from God, I had to renounce those things and order them out of my life. Only by the power of God in me could I do that. Was I finally ready for this deliverance?

With the same resolve it took to forgive others, I now pled with God to deliver me. The following journal entry is one of many that record my petitions for deliverance:

> Father, I have believed a lie. I have accepted a false identity. I have believed I need to be perfect to receive Your love. I'm so sorry. I don't feel lovable. But I choose to believe the truth of Your love for me. You loved me so much You gave Your Son to die for me so You could draw close to me and so I could have a personal relationship with You. I have known and believed that in my heart. I have given my life to You, but now I realize I've believed Satan's lies about myself rather than Your truth of me. You love me unconditionally. I don't deserve such love, but the truth of Your Word says You do love me unreservedly, passionately. I choose to believe You and turn away from Satan's lies. Please forgive me for believing the lie. Help me to overcome my unbelief and live in the light of Your truth. My identity is in You.

The process of deliverance from sins, which weigh down the soul, continues throughout life. As never before, I longed to give up completely anything separating me from Jesus.

God began to speak to my spirit about my need to confess the false identities as sin. First, they took up space in my soul, which God wanted to occupy, and second, because I accepted them. Even though I subconsciously took on guilt emanating from the end-of-life decisions, I still needed to confess the false identity of guilt and ask for forgiveness, allowing God to lift this burden and replace it with His grace.

As God brought them to my mind, I confessed every false identity individually and admitted I'd allowed each to enter my soul. I surrendered them all and asked God to forgive me and to take them from me. Then I asked God to replace each false identity with a specific attribute of His.

Today, those negative forces no longer wield power over me. When they threaten to enter my thoughts, I recognize them early and don't dwell on them. I focus on God's love for me and move on. My new identity helps me sense God's presence.

Several of my journal entries reflect how patiently the Lord dealt with me during this process:

> I must not allow my emotions to dictate who I am.
>
> I feel rejected ... I am rejected. This is a lie. That is not my identity in Christ.
>
> I am His (Christ's) Beloved.
>
> I'm sorry, Lord, for allowing this identity to dictate who I am, how I act and feel. Please forgive me.
>
> I rebuke the false identity of rejection and ask You to replace it in the name of Jesus with 'I am Your Beloved.'
>
> The Lord holds me very close. He longs to be near me, spending time with me."

[*Another journal entry*]

> Father, forgive me for my wrong choices.
>
> Take these false identities from me as I repent in dust and ashes.
>
> Replace depression with a spirit that rejoices in Your presence.
>
> Replace self-pity with humility and freedom to love others.

Replace unforgiveness with grace, longsuffering, patience, and kindness.

Replace resentment with a realization that I have all I need in You.

Replace bitterness with sweetness, the sweetness of a heart filled with Your Holy Spirit and the ability to love You and experience You on a much deeper level.

Coping Strategies

- Practice the discipline of quietness before God: Spend time, not only studying the Scriptures and praying, but also being still before God, quietly allowing Him to speak His truth to your heart.

- Detox: Ask God to change your toxic thought patterns and exchange them for His life-giving thoughts.

  → Acknowledge the lies. Ask God to reveal the lies you have believed about yourself and others. Ask God to show you any false identities that you have allowed to control you, such as bitterness, anger, fear, guilt, and perfectionism.

  → Confess the lies and ask God to forgive you for believing them: Stand against the lies and false identities according to the directions outlined in Ephesians 6.

  → Seek God's truth: Ask God to speak His truth into your situation and relationships.

  → Walk in God's truth: Ask God to remove any false identities and to replace them with His nature. Ask Him to give you His thoughts so that you can think and act in agreement with your true identity as a child of God.

CHAPTER 27

Rescued by
His Love

*If you are going to move forward, if you are going to
participate in the life God imagined when He thought of you,
... you must run with everything you have into the strong
arms of God and let His perfect love drive out every fear.*[51]

Angela Thomas from *Do You Think I'm Beautiful?*

Sweetly, tenderly, God called me to deeper levels of intimacy.
I asked the Holy Spirit to interpret the Scriptures and open my
heart to receive more of His love. The Scriptures had always been
important to me. Now His words became my sustenance. As my
body needed strength for each day, similarly my soul needed a constant supply of His grace and joy, a daily supply of the Holy Spirit's
strength and renewal. I wanted to hold all other relationships loosely
but have my identity anchored to God's love.

Angela Thomas's book *Do You Think I'm Beautiful?* awakened
within me an unquenchable thirst to drink deeply of God's love. As
I worked through the book's companion journal and meditated on
the Scriptures, I soaked in the love of Christ and began to grasp the
depth and richness of His love for me. I wept. I poured myself out,
and He poured His love in, love that flowed from a living fountain
quenching my parched soul. God bathed me in His love.

Yet, I longed to grow even more in love with Him and embrace
His love as my most valued treasure.

As I relinquished my desires and surrendered more of myself to Christ, He planted the seeds of His nature in me, and that which began to grow and bear fruit was of Him, not of me. I began to allow His love to guide my words, actions, thoughts, and motives. In turn, fear, perfectionism, pride, and striving occupied less room in my life.

I allowed His love to fill and rule over me, and He gave me confidence that Jesus Christ lived in me through His Holy Spirit and interceded for me before God. People disappoint. Life disappoints. God replaced my disappointments with hope—hope that He'd renew me, fill me to overflowing, and redeem my life, my loss, with His love.

I became more passionate about my time alone in God's presence, which began to directly affect my attitude and feelings toward my husband. According to statistics, only a small fraction of marriages survives the loss of a child. Yet, today our marriage prevails—stronger than ever.

God didn't fix my marriage. He changed me.

God showed me His love for Ronnie and increased my own love for my husband, my acceptance of him, and of myself. God made me more appreciative of Ronnie's expressions of love and strengthened my commitment to him. Since I no longer dwelt on anger, bitterness, and resentment toward him, we enjoyed more peace together. My husband also began to express his love and appreciation for me more tenderly than he had in the past, and I began to accept his love more graciously. When I learned of God's passion for me, I became less needful of Ronnie's attention or approval. I realized God desires me and wants to spend time with me even though I am far from perfect. My happiness and contentment, once dependent upon my feelings or upon the actions, attitudes, or words of others, now had a new source: my identity in Christ.

Gratitude for God's provisions and newfound hope in Christ unlocked the key to my heart, so I could enjoy the fruit of God's fellowship. I surrendered my selfish desire to use my time in my own way. Instead, I passionately sought time with Christ. To my surprise, where I once resented Ronnie's absences, I now anticipated them as precious time alone with God.

Gradually, God taught me to persevere in my commitment to Him, not in my work for Him. I needed Him to remind me constantly not to measure His affection for me by my works but by His identity in me. I repeatedly told myself, "God is Love. He loves me."

When I gave myself to God and loved Him above all others, I felt a greater sense of His presence in my life. His love for me became more real. When I allowed Him to be strong in me and I relinquished control to Him, I found my center, my peace, in Him. My faith in Jesus became my lifeline. He imparted His thoughts and wisdom to apply to my life's circumstances. He gave me hope and strength for the day's trials and renewed my energy for the day's work.

To my amazement, the more I relinquished to the Lord, the more joy-filled freedom I experienced! Christ had died to free me from the tyranny of my negativity. When I allowed freedom in Christ to rule in me, my identity flowed from His love. I wanted to walk step-by-step in that freedom. His steadfast love called me to live and move in my identity in Christ, not intermittently, but unceasingly.

I discovered my greatest enemy was not those who opposed me or who stood in judgment of me. My greatest enemy was myself. For a long time I didn't realize my error. I had been listening to voices other than those of my Savior for years, including my own voice, my self-loathing, even my propensity to punish myself.

Confessing this sin, gradually I learned to shut out all other voices and only listen to God. He convinced me of His love and His concern for me and the length to which He had gone, and would go, to take care of my needs. He went to the farthest lengths, the death of His one and only Son, to ensure He could hold me close, protect me, and comfort me. My heart swelled to take in the reality: Jesus Christ broke down the barrier between us. He alone made me complete, whole, and perfect in God's eyes.

I began to realize how wide, how long, how deep, and how high His love is for me. His love stretches wider than the chasm created by my sin. It lasts longer than my life on this earth or my daughter's life. It reaches deeper than the depths of depression into which I had crawled and lifts me from my heart's ashes to the heights of heaven's joy. God's love is higher than my mind can fathom (Ephesians

3:18–19). When I focused on His love for me in this way, I knew nothing could separate me from the love of God embodied in Christ Jesus (Romans 8:39).

He knew me better than anyone else did. Was I finally ready to entrust my whole life to God?

God broke through my self-condemning thoughts. I realized how weak I was, and am, and always will be, in comparison to God's strength and power. He never wanted me to depend on my own strength, but rather for *Him* to be strong *in* me. This was the highest good God intended for me. I never could have done it all. That's not what He cared about. He cared about me. I stopped trying to be strong. I leaned strong into Him.

God rescued me. He came quietly and whispered peace and deliverance to my heart. My experience was just as powerful as if the gallant Prince of Peace, the King of kings, arrived on a galloping white stallion, broke down the prison walls, whisked me to the safety of His embrace, and we rode off together into an eternity of love.

I know in this life there's no fairy tale ending, no happily ever after. Nevertheless, when I finally hit bottom, there He stood, shining bright and beautiful in the robe of His perfection, ready to cover my imperfection. When Jesus arrived this time, I didn't cower in fear or recoil in reflection of my sin. He vanquished my fears, captured my heart, and satisfied my hungering soul in the passion of His redeeming love.

I realized I'd never be able to live the perfect life I relentlessly tried to live. Still, God created me to be loved by Him and to share His love with others. Although I could never be good enough to earn His love, I've been justified by faith in the work of Christ:

(I) have peace with God through our Lord Jesus Christ, through whom also (I) have access by faith into this grace in which (I) stand, and rejoice in hope of the glory of God. And not only that, but (I) also glory in (my) tribulations, knowing that tribulation produces perseverance; and perseverance, character; and character, hope. Now hope does not disappoint, because the love of God has been poured in (my heart) by the Holy Spirit who was given to [me]. (Romans 5:1–5, KJV)

Armed with the power of His Holy Spirit as my guide and the joy of the Lord as my strength, I gradually left behind my former ideas, my old identity, and assumed my new identity as one bound in love to Christ. When I honor God above all others and listen to His voice above all others, He pours out His mercy to me, pours His blessing upon me, and I can love myself as He loves me. In turn, I can love others as I love myself by drawing from His fountain of love within me.

God showed me He never stopped loving me, nor would He ever love me any less because of the choices I made throughout my life. His undying love for me compelled Him to give His life for me, to empty me out through this experience and now, to fill me with the fullness of His love (Ephesians 3:19).

The miracle of this newfound level of intimacy goes from joy to greater joy and faith to greater faith. The new path He has for me, the better way, is not always the easy road to take. There are still times I fail to reflect Christ's holiness in my actions or attitude. Momentarily, I may focus too much on the acceptance or rejection of others, slipping back into the deception of perfectionism. Nevertheless, God doesn't punish me at those times. Christ already took the punishment for me. His death is the gate through which I gain access to God.

When I remember how much He loves me, I don't need the love of others to fulfill my need for intimacy and worth. In turn, my need to achieve perfection in every aspect of my life diminishes. My capacity and desire to love unconditionally and to serve others selflessly increases.

God continues to heal me of my need for acceptance from others by continuing to reveal even greater depths of His great love for me. According to the love described in 1 Corinthians 13, I must rid my heart of its self-centered desires daily, so He can pour in His perfect love. When I allow His love to flow out of me through my thoughts, actions, and motives, I live, breathe, and have my being in Him. In this way, I abide in Christ, and Christ abides in me.

He protects me. He will not allow me to wander beyond His reach. Now I realize when I walk away from Him, He responds with mercy. I no longer fear losing His love because His love in me casts out fear. When I inevitably stumble, I don't fear falling from His grace; instead, I know I'll be caught and held in Christ's loving embrace.

He draws me back and woos me with tender words: *"Believe in My love for you. Simply accept My love for you, My unconditional, strong, perfect, unfailing love for you, My child."*

I've found that when hardships seem insurmountable, depression, fear, and anxiety threaten to steal my joy. Yet, God sees into the human heart. He understands what we face each day. In all of those losses, desperate, alone, and at the end of our resources, God remains faithful. Even when we shut Him out or neglect to acknowledge His presence and power, He never leaves us. We just fail to focus on Him. He waits patiently until, once again, we come to the end of ourselves, and then He fills us as a gentle breeze fills the air, as one rekindles dying embers, blowing gently to revive their flame. Likewise, God's holy flame, the Holy Spirit, burns within me.

God alone can fill the void in our lives. He alone can open eyes to see His good plan for us and give us courage to walk into new life. He invites us to begin each day anew with Him.

I need to take the time to sit quietly with the Lord every single day. The days I fail to do so, I often struggle with my identity in Christ and my identity as a person, wife, and mother. Prayer and meditation on His Word help to keep Christ on the throne of my heart, placing all others, including myself, in their rightful position. Remembering that Christ alone determines my identity and value releases me from the bondage of my "works" and the drive to do everything perfectly.

God calls me to freedom, not works; to love, not punishment; to relationship, not fear. Christ is full of compassion. His tears mingle with ours because He understands our losses. He, too, loved my daughter. He *loves* her even more than I do. Standing on the other side of this tragedy, I rejoice knowing that my daughter is in heaven where she now lives in the joy of God's presence. In the midst of this great loss, I now possess peace and joy that's beyond understanding. This is freedom, fully realized and experienced. He says, *"I love you, my darling. I love you with an everlasting love. My love for you will never change. It has nothing to do with how you are performing."*

Although I had mapped out my life, I now see I hadn't arrived anywhere. I could only find the path to God by following the way of Christ and by putting to death those things standing between us. He had planned and directed this journey. Gloriously, I ended up finding myself along the way.

As I struggled along the path of this journey, there were those who wanted me to "get over it" and "move on." "We want the old Nancy back." However, God wanted so much more for me. In fact, I couldn't be the old me. This tragedy changed me. God had something much better in mind—the abundant life of joy made possible through Christ.

God searched my heart. He knew my imperfections. In spite of my sin, He declared His love for me.

He only asks us to love Him. I did. I loved Him with all my heart. I still do. I discovered God is happiest when I lose myself in Him, which makes me happiest of all.

I had reached the end of my journey. Or is it the end? He continues to serenade me with His love song.

———◆———

Coping Strategies

- Admit your weaknesses: Accept God's sufficiency.
- Admit your failures: Accept God's forgiveness.
- Admit your fears: Accept God's love.
- Let God's perfect love drive out your fears.

CHAPTER 28

Revelations of His Love

The place that Jesus takes in our soul, he shall never remove from it without end … he wants our heart to be raised mightily above the deepness of the earth and all vain sorrows and rejoice in him … oneing itself to him in rest and peace by his grace.[52]

Julian of Norwich from *Revelation of Love*

Asking God why everything happened the way it did sometimes sidetracked me from learning the lessons of love He had for me through this experience. From the outset, God determined how this ordeal would unfold. Not until He finished His work did it finally end. I simply needed to trust His timing and His wisdom.

Author Philip Yancey says, "By focusing too myopically on what we want God to do on our behalf, we may miss the significance of what he has already done."[53] Many blessings[54] were overshadowed by the one huge miracle I wanted for Stacey and for myself—her healing.

It helps to look back to fully benefit from His life lessons, to glean the good from tragedy, and to allow the soul to be enlarged because of it rather than diminished by it. More than once I asked God, "Why this way?" Perhaps God knew I couldn't bear the shock of losing my daughter instantly. I needed to let go of her little by little instead of all at once.

In Beth Moore's book, *Believing God*, she voices my own question: "Couldn't there have been an easier way? Finally and sadly, I accepted the answer: apparently not. My God loves me too much not to have chosen another way if it would have sufficed."[55]

I believe God allows hardship to come to His children. Moreover, I agree with pastor and author Tony Evans who says:

> Those are the times when He wants to break you ... to bring you to the end of your own resources, so you'll say, 'I can't.' There's an experience of God that we can get in no other way than through the pain He allows in our lives. And when you wonder why He allows the pain to last so long, it's because He's trying to take you deeper."[56]

"The Lord isn't slow to do what he promised as some people think. Rather, he is patient for [our] sake. He doesn't want to destroy anyone but wants all [of us] to have an opportunity to turn to him and change the way [we] think and act ... " so we reflect the beautiful characteristics of His nature (2 Peter 3:9, GWT).

Long after Stacey died, I considered another reason her death may have happened the way it did. God used this journey to undergird and augment my belief in His goodness. God allowed me to go only so far in my grief before He pulled me out of the depths and gave me a reprieve. Otherwise, I might have immersed myself in my sorrow, unable to return to the reality of the here and now, the stuff of today requiring my attention.

We must each choose how we respond to loss and how we allow it to affect our future. We can stoically endure the hardship and allow it to diminish us by becoming bitter, angry, or assuming any number of other destructive reactions. Or, like clay in a potter's hand, we can choose to be malleable by learning from the experience and allowing it to enlarge our soul.

God may have had a number of reasons why it happened as it did. I rest now in the assurance of His wisdom in the way Stacey's death unfolded.

I remember sitting on the dock, reading the history of Esther on the day of Stacey's accident. Just as God chose the meek Jewish maiden, Hadassah, to become Queen Esther for a unique time and purpose, God chooses *each* of His children to take part in His story. His eternal story unfolds within the realm of this world and encompasses all of the Heavenlies. I wondered why God created me. What was my purpose in His narrative?

Mankind's redemption, made possible by faith in Christ's sacrifice, is God's glorious theme. He wants to redeem our losses. In redemption, we see who God is. He invites us all to become part of His story of redemption.

I am part of that story. God placed me in His story at a specific time for His appointed purpose. I met Him on the day He first opened my eyes to His majesty and wonder. He drew me to Himself. On the day of my daughter's accident, He orchestrated the most defining period of my life. God would not let this chapter of my life be wasted. In God's strength, as I yoked myself to Him, I carried the load, not all loads, but only that which He planned for me to bear. Any strength I exhibited, God had already established in me in preparation for "such a time as this" (Esther 4:14). In this way, *in His way,* He lightened my burden, and I found my joy in His strength.

He carried my daughter into His throne room to spend eternity in His presence. He carried me into the sanctuary of His love to renew my life. Today I tell the story of His good purpose and His great love—love not just for my daughter, not just for me, but for all humanity. "For God loved the world so much that He gave His one and only Son so that everyone who believes in him will not perish but will have eternal life" (John 3:16, NLT). He desires His children as much, even more, than we desire Him!

God created our physical bodies with the capacity to hold roughly ten gallons of water, ten pints of blood, and 25 trillion red blood cells. However, He left a God-sized hole in our souls, a chasm only He can fill.

We can never attain complete and full satisfaction apart from God. The Master Designer intended to fill our emptiness with the measure of all the fullness of Himself. Just as air fills a vacuum, when we trust Jesus Christ with our lives, God's Spirit rushes in. He fills the vacuum within our gasping souls. God's love filled empty places in me I didn't even know existed.

Like water bubbles from a fountain, the joy of the Lord flows from my soul. Jesus Christ, the Living Water, provides an inexhaustible resource of God's love. My fountains flow from Him (Psalm 87:7). Gratitude opens the faucet of His unfailing love.

I bow down, not as a cowering outcast, but as one who is known completely by the One who loves me completely. I may not be able to understand so grand and great a love, but I can still abide in it. God ultimately healed my broken heart, turned me from my unhealthy and unrighteous ways, and turned my sorrows into joy.

It seems so very long ago.

In the early spring after Stacey died, I worried about meeting her when I got to Heaven. Would I be able to face her? Would she be angry with me? Stacey quietly reassured me, not in an audible voice, but to my spirit: *"How could I be angry with you? You released me into my Father's hands. I'm okay, Mom."* She let me know she was with God. She knew I did the best I could to take care of her.

I thank God for assuring me Stacey lives in heaven with Him. By the grace of God, I live, breathe, and have my being in Him. One day I too will dwell in the presence of my Savior where my daughter has gone before me.

This hallowed experience taught me the excellence of His love. It was a gift of knowledge from His Holy Spirit, made possible through the greatest loss I have ever experienced, the death of our child. From the vantage point of the deepest valley of guilt, the darkest season of grief, God's love sustained me throughout the journey.

By His tender mercy, the morning light from heaven broke upon me and shattered the darkness. I found the path of peace (Luke 1:77–79). God rescued Stacey through death's door and carried her soul through Heaven's gates (2 Timothy 4:18). He rescued me from the stygian shadows of my life. He delivered Stacey *from* her peril. He delivered me *through* my peril. God delivers His sheep from the "Valley of the Shadow of Death." I saw the Son rise over the mountaintop. My journey ended. Finally home, I ran to the embrace of the Lover of my soul. I ran as one made new, as one redeemed.

Run! Run, I say to you. Run with all your strength, with all your heart, and with all you have within you into His outspread arms. Behold the wounded flesh. Remember. Drink deeply from the blood poured out for you.[57] Satisfy the longing of your soul. Commune with Him in whom love is perfect, in whom union is complete, and in whom bliss is everlasting.

> Trust in the LORD and do good; dwell in the land and enjoy safe pasture. Delight yourself in the LORD and he will give you the desires of your heart. Commit your way to the LORD; trust in him and he will do this: He will make your righteousness shine like the dawn, the justice of your cause like the noonday sun. Be still before the LORD and wait patiently for him. (Psalm 37:3–7, NIV)

I testify to God's grace here on earth and Stacey testifies in Heaven that He saves us only by His grace. "To the praise of the glory of his grace, wherein he hath made us accepted in the beloved" (Ephesians 1:6, KJV).

> Now to Him who is able to keep you from stumbling,
> And to present you faultless
> Before the presence of His glory with exceeding joy,
> To God our Savior,
> Who alone is wise,
> Be glory and majesty,
> Dominion and power,
> Both now and forever.
> Amen.
> (Jude 24–25, NKJV)

Coping Strategies

- Ask God to redeem your loss as you:

    → Depend on God's strength, not your own.

    → Seek and trust God's wisdom, not your own.

    → Believe God's truth about you.

    → Release your fear of losing God's grace and embrace freedom in Christ.

    → Ask God to exchange your guilt, grief, and fear for His forgiveness, joy, and perfect love.

The Pilgrimage—
True North to Home

In beautiful things St. Francis saw Beauty itself, and
through His vestiges imprinted on creation he followed
his Beloved everywhere, making from all things a
ladder by which he could climb up and embrace Him
who is utterly desirable.[58]

St. Bonventure, speaking of St. Francis

Years sped past since the illuminating autumn morning in 1993 when God etched a picture of His Presence within me. Over those harrowing weeks, I took "the road less traveled" to the medical center and home again many times.

I still drive the same country road, which led me to Stacey's bedside day after day in what seemed like another lifetime. Thousands of moments have left traces of footprints upon my life, written as wrinkles weathered and spoken as bones creaking.

On one particular spring morning, the Lord spoke again. Light answered. As I drove down the well-worn dirt road, He revealed even greater depths of His love for me and of His providential care over my life, over the entire world.

Beams of sunlight appeared like ladders stretching from Heaven to earth. I put the car in park and left the motor running. That particular morning no one waited at the hospital for me. I had no reason to hurry. I walked into the center of this Heavenly portal and immersed myself in light.

Taking a few steps forward, awestruck by the nearness of the sun's shimmering rays, I reached out. I pulled back. Reached again. With my hand, I carressed the light. Or did the light caress me?

I *felt* the light. It patterned across my hand … striped with warm, vibrant color interspersed with cold dullness. The pattern superimposed itself across the surface of my skin.

Transfixed, the scene unraveled before me.

Ephemeral vapor draped the pristine woodlands, permeated physical substance. I felt as transient as the limb-dripping molecules of hydrogen and oxygen collecting on spring's virgin growth, revitalizing the carpet of hairy moss below.

I stood—awestruck—in the middle of the road, searching for God's "vestiges imprinted on creation."[59] Behind me, I heard a dissonant sound that was unnatural and foreign to the chattering creatures scurrying about. The car's engine whirred. It grated against the harmony of the stream's babbling and the leaves' rustling.

I turned to silence the engine and looked up the road. The rays of sun disappeared. I saw only crystal-clear air. I turned again and gazed down the road. From this vantage point, I could *see* the air, its composition profuse with material substance. Countless particles of dust, matter, and vapor danced in the beams of sunlight.

With a turn of the key, silence.

Bathed in God's presence, He sang to me with notes floating sweetly on the wind of His breath. In addition to God's divine revelation of Himself through the Bible, the Creator of all reveals Himself through nature. Often He is felt, like a powerful, frightening force. Sometimes He's sensed like a soft whisper.

On that special day, God unveiled my mind. He unstopped my ears. I perceived Him all around me in all I heard, saw, touched, *even* tasted in the damp air. Heaven's King drew near! I breathed Him in as I breathed in the clean, crisp morning. I breathed in His Presence. He awakened every element of my being. As I beheld the earthy substance suspended in sunlight, Eternity pulled off the sheet concealing His Omnipresence and exposed the heavenly filament alive with His Spirit. He unveiled His Transcendence.

God penetrates and sustains everything.

Again I reached out. I felt the warmth of the ray of sun sent millions of miles from its source. I felt the warmth of God's heart touching mine, and I realized I not only stood in His presence in that moment of time and space, the God-lesson ran much deeper.

Some circumstances of this life may obscure God's presence momentarily, just as something as elusive as water vapor can completely conceal a twist in the road. When the fog dissipates, I see more clearly. Now I see the unexpected twist in life had led me deeper into His grace. God's grace grows more evident to my soul, as does His enduring Presence, in spite of, or perhaps because of, the temporary disorientation.

The darkness of this world may conceal His Presence. The darkness of my earthy flesh sometimes conceals His light within me. Other times, I may be magnificently undone by the manifestation of His holiness. "His countenance [is like] the sun shining in its strength" (Revelation 1:16, AKJV). At those moments, I can only fall at His feet and invoke His mercy upon my sin-stained soul. I wait for the touch of His hand to lift me. I implore, "What do You want me to do, Lord?"

Walking among the fog-filled stratus hanging over the valleys that etch the earth's surface and breathing in the deceptive smog of this "fallen world" may sometimes cloud my mind and diminish me. Words slip easily over my tongue: "Father, if You are willing, take this cup from me." Others stick to the roof of my mouth like cement: "Yet, not my will, but yours be done" (Luke 22:42, NIV).

Meanwhile, I walk in the shadow of this world beneath the Holy Heavenly City, which has "no need of the sun, neither of the moon, to shine in it, for the glory of God did lighten it, and the Lamb is the light thereof" (Revelation 21:23, KJV). The same light, which now illuminates me, shines from my daughter, who gazes upon His glorious radiance from Heaven's vantage point! The light of His Presence dissipates the darkness around me as surely as the sun's rays stretch from Heaven to earth, separating day from night.

God exists outside the bounds of time. Yet, at just the right moment, He sends His light to illumine my present path. He charted my life's course as He charts the heavenlies with fixed celestial orbs of light. He walked with me from my beginning, promising never to leave my side. He vows to escort me through Eternity's gates:

> The Lord will come from Heaven with a command ... the dead who believed in Christ will come back to life. Then, together with them, we [who have answered the call of Christ and are] still alive will be taken in the clouds to meet the Lord in the air. In this way we will always be with the Lord? (1 Thessalonians 4:16–17, GWT)

The infinitude of God cannot be encapsulated or limited by matter as can we who wear the flesh and blood of humanity. Yet, at one time, He did put on flesh. His veins flowed. The Divine confined within frail humanity. He became my Brother. The God-man became the Pilgrim of His world. While a pilgrim on this earth, Christ secured my future home within His celestial temple. The great mystery is that my body is His temple even now. I carry Him within me. *He* carries *me* within His breast.

Just as light is invisible until something is suspended within its path, air is invisible, impalpable, unnoticed until it is put in motion. Then we call it wind. I call Him *Breath of Heaven*. I breathe in the wind of His Holy Spirit.

I stand upon hallowed ground with heart bowed, a simple country road where the light of a Holy God enlightens my dark soul. My spirit has no true home in this world. I, too, am a pilgrim. I look for God not only in that which is visible but also among the unseen things beneath the surface of this world's enigmatic beauty and its temporary troubles. I roam about earth's countryside while on my way to another place. I am "a soul in progress toward a very specific and elusive goal," as was Teresa of Avila, who accepted that "her sinful human nature would keep pulling her off course and that only faith, calibrated by grace, could put her back on the road to God."[60]

The veins of my life's path ultimately carry me back to the heart of God. He wastes nothing in my life's pilgrimage. I will not settle for the wilderness of this world, no matter how majestic is the creation nor how precious the gifts this world confers. God offers something far better—the gift of Himself and the promised land of eternity with Him, the sacred place upon which all the dotted points, wherein I now perceive His presence, will someday converge into One. His glory will fill the space between the skies. My heart longs for that country infinitely more beautiful, and intrinsically more real, than that which my eyes can see, my hands can touch, and my ears can hear.

I have turned from the shadows of desolation and depression. I've become a stranger in this place. I've determined to follow His light until I reach the mansion He prepared for me, the one filled with all of Himself.

God zigzags across my life like a needle picking up a tiny thread connecting fabric to fabric. Only He connects me to Himself— physical to mystical. The soul now dwelling within my finite earthy tent has become a living stone seamed into His eternal temple.

The mystery of His unseen Presence follows me throughout my course over every gnarled and craggy path. He guides me through the fog and mist, which envelope this firmament. He shines into me, so wherever I stand in the Son's hazy shadow or amid His blazing brilliance, whatever life has brought or still may hold, I see He has been with me. He is with me. He will be with me—now and forever.

And we walk on.

Coping Strategies

- Make a conscious, concerted effort to "see" the ways in which God has revealed His love through this trauma.
- Make a list of God's revelations of His love to you.

RESOURCES

www.caringbridge.org

www.rmhcny.org

www.stephenministries.org

Research resources available in print or on the Internet include
Frank H. Netter, MD's *Atlas of Human Anatomy; Oxford Learner's Dictionary; Stedman's Medical Dictionary*

emedicine.medscape.com

http://www.hopkinsmedicine.org/healthlibrary

www.assertivepatient.org/patient-advocate.html

http://www.mikelavere.com/healthcare-2/insurance-companies-dictating-quality-care/ (last viewed 9/19/2016.)

www.griefshare.org

www.compassionatefriends.org

National Suicide Prevention Lifeline-1–800–273–8255;
Text "GO" or "START" to 741741

The Search for Significance, Robert S. McGee, Thomas Nelson Publishers,
ISBN-10: 0-8499-4424-4
ISBN-13: 978-0-8499-4424-6

The Grief Recovery Handbook, John W. James and Russell Friedman,
Collins Living Publishers, www.grief.net

Medical References

GLASGOW COMA SCALE

The Glasgow Coma Scale (GCS) defines the severity of a traumatic brain injury (TBI) within 48 hours of injury.

Eye opening
See the list below:

Spontaneous = 4
To speech = 3
To painful stimulation = 2
No response = 1

Motor response
See the list below:

Follows commands = 6
Makes localizing movements to pain = 5
Makes withdrawal movements to pain = 4
Flexor (decorticate) posturing to pain = 3
Extensor (decerebrate) posturing to pain = 2
No response = 1

Verbal response
See the list below:

Oriented to person, place, and date = 5
Converses but is disoriented = 4
Says inappropriate words = 3
Says incomprehensible sounds = 2
No response = 1

The severity of TBI according to the GCS score (within 48 h) is as follows:

Severe TBI = 3–8
Moderate TBI = 9–12
Mild TBI = 13–15

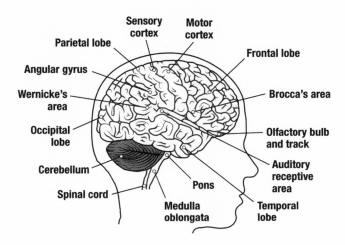

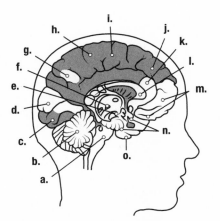

a. **Brain stem, Pontine, midbrain, dorsal mesencephalon**

b. **Cerebellum**
   Motion perception

c. **Primary Visual Cortex**

d. **Visual Association Cortex**
   Creates imagery associations with internal information being processed

e. **Hypothalamus**

f. **Thalamus**

g. **Rt Inferior Parietal Cortex**
   Spatial organization (fictive dream space), distinction between self and others, metaphor processing

h. **Precuneus**
   Episodic memory

i. **Primary Motor and Sensory Cortex (I/O Blocked)**

j. **Dorsolateral PFC**
   Rational linear thought

k. **Anterior Cingulate**
   Mediates conflicting perceptions and projects possible resolutions, selects rewarding outcomes

l. **Basal Ganglion**
   Learning and behavior control, motivation toward eventual rather than immediate reward, Novelty decision making

m. **Frontal Cortex**
   Self-awareness, sense of knowing, goal directed reward motivated planning and decision organization

n. **Limbic Sys and Amygdala**
   Emotion and memory processing, associates emotion with sensory input, emotional value judgement

o. **Temporal**
   Visual and audio processing, perception and recognition

The Way of Pain

A s I walked through *my* valley, the following testimony helped me put aside false and destructive behaviors and thoughts. With them behind me, I could move ahead into that which is true and right as I searched for my identity. The following testimony helped to keep me on track.

The Way of Pain
by Kit Jackson

Search me, O God and know my heart, try me and know my anxious thoughts, and see if there be any hurtful way (literal translation is the "way of pain" from the Hebrew "osteb") *in me, and lead me in the everlasting way.*

(Psalm 139:23–24)

The Lord gives you rest from your pain ("osteb") *and turmoil.*

(Isaiah 14:3)

Several years ago, I had a dream in which I was looking in a mirror. My face reflected back dark hollows where my cheekbones should have been, somewhat like a negative for a photo. I asked the Lord what this meant. He told me that's how I saw myself. I had tried to empty myself and serve others to the point I no longer seemed to have anything left and had lost sight of my true identity in the Lord. I felt somehow like a "battered" child of God, and, yet, I knew in my heart He had never hurt me. (Isa. 53:4: "Surely our griefs He himself bore, and our sorrows [pains] He carried.") But I had been hurt many times. If I really admitted who I felt I was, I probably would have said, "I am hurt."

God began to show me that, because I felt I had "innocently" been hurt, even though I had forgiven those who hurt me, I soaked up the hurts like a big sponge and allowed them to accumulate in my soul rather than holding up my shield of faith to extinguish the fiery darts and keep them out. (Ephesians 6:16). That was keeping me from being the person God wanted me to be—truly free in Him. (Colossians 3:3: " ... Your life is hidden with Christ in God.")

The Father identifies Himself as "I AM" in His Word (Exodus 3:14). Our "I am," or identity, is in the area of the soul (intellect, emotions, and will)— the thinking, feeling part of our being, which Christ laid down His soul to save. Isaiah 53:10 states, "If He [lit. "His soul"] would render Himself as a guilt offering, He will see His offspring ... "

First Peter 1:9 speaks of the relationship of one's faith to the soul: "obtaining as the outcome of your faith the salvation of your souls." I knew Jesus was fully capable of healing and delivering my soul, as well, so I began to realize I had sinned against God by holding on to my "innocent hurt" and by allowing it to take over my being.

The same can be true of anger held (Ephesians 4:26) or bitterness allowed to take root (Hebrews 12:15). Of course, we're going to feel hurt (which can lead to a progression of rejection, resentment, and then rebellion) or anger or bitterness at times. However, it's when we retain these negative responses, they become sin. It became clear that the only way to get rid of all the accumulated grief and pain and sorrow was to confess their retention as sin and ask God to forgive me and lift it from me.

Around the same time, we attended a charismatic meeting in which a husband and wife team ministered. One of the areas the wife emphasized, especially for women, included the persistent use of prayer language and, in our personal worship, praying slowly in the Spirit to slow down our racing minds and anxious thoughts and help us rest in God. I went forward for prayer later, and the woman had a word for me, in part, telling me I suffered from a negative self-image. (Of course, I immediately remembered my dream. I hadn't told her about any of this. God used her to confirm what He had told me). She told me God was healing me and, as part of the process, she instructed me to listen to and write down what those who loved me in the body of Christ said about me for the next couple of weeks. I completed the list and could hardly believe how much more positive their view appeared compared to the negative picture I'd had of myself and the importance of the body of Christ in showing me my real role in Jesus.

I can't overemphasize the importance of admitting that holding the hurt was a sin. I had to be convinced that it didn't glorify God, and I had not made use of the shield of faith to get rid of the hurts before they became a part of me. (Romans 14:23: " … whatever is not from faith is sin.")

Jesus asked the man by the pool of Bethesda, "Do you wish to get well?" It was hard to lay down a false identity that had been with me so long, especially since I had felt "innocent" in taking it on. It had virtually taken over. However, when I confessed my guilt and my need for forgiveness and allowed God to lift the burden of the hurt, He set me free and started to reveal my true identity in Him.

Remember, this process can apply to any false identity you've taken on— not just "hurt." After you've confessed having invited a false identity to enter your soul and asked God to forgive you and lift it from you, it's important to ask Him to fill you instead with good things from Him. Be specific. Examples include the fruits of Spirit such as "love, joy, peace, patience, kindness, goodness, gentleness, faithfulness, and self-control" (Galatians 5:22–23).

God promises "they will not hurt or destroy in all My holy mountain, for the earth will be full of the knowledge of the Lord as the waters cover the sea" (Isaiah 11:9). "Every good thing bestowed and every perfect gift is from above, coming down from the Father of lights, with Whom there is no variation or shifting shadow" (James 1:17).

Revelations of His Love

You meant evil against me, but God meant it for good in order to bring about this present result

(Genesis 50:20)

And we know that God causes all things to work together for good to those who love God, to those who are called according to His purpose.

(Romans 8:28, NLT)

And my God will supply all your needs according to His riches in glory in Christ Jesus.

(Philippians 4:19)

I'm grateful for the *many* miracles and blessings I failed to see earlier. Desiring the one huge miracle of Stacey's healing clouded my awareness of the numerous miracles God provided along the way.

The following provides a partial list of specific times God revealed His love and intervened on our behalf. Only God knows of the countless other experiences of His grace and provision for us during this journey. I thank God and praise Him for the loving kindness He bestowed upon us during this trauma and the many blessings He continues to shower upon us.

1. While in Ontario, Ronnie was the first person to speak to the hospital staff. (Chapter 1)

2. The EMT and Life Flight teams successfully transported Stacey from the accident scene to Hobson Medical Center. (Chapter 8)

3. We traveled from Canada to Hershey in spite of the blown tire on the boat trailer and arrived at the hospital precisely at God's appointed time. (Chapter 1)

4. John believed Stacey squeezed his hand when he asked her if she was saved; thus, he perceived that she communicated affirmatively—not verbally—but in the way God chose. (Chapter 4)

5. The surgery to keep Stacey alive succeeded. She lived sixty-eight days. (Chapters 1, 21)

6. Stacey survived transport from Hobson to Grayson Medical Center in spite of the thunderstorm. (Chapter 8)

7. The result of the move caused by the insurance struggle meant Stacey relocated only fifteen miles from home rather than three hours. (Chapter 8)

8. The same day I got the red roses for Stacey, Pastor Louis Hoffman arrived to pray the verse from Matthew 16:19, which confirmed for me where she would spend eternity and probably released her spirit. (Chapter 16)

9. I had a host of support from family, friends, pastors, counselors, elders, and even strangers. (Throughout)

10. The letter from Joni arrived *after* the fleece had been cast and answered, so while the decision to remove the hydration and nutrition became more emotionally difficult to work through, it had already been made. (Chapters 18, 20)

11. Joni took the call from my brother Steven, listened to his explanation, and reversed her earlier position. Supportive and caring, she ministered to me many times over the years. (Chapter 20)

12. Stacey continued to breathe on her own for twenty-six days after the staff removed the ventilator, so God continued to answer my earlier prayer of "Breathe, Stace, breathe." (Chapters 1, 21)

13. Days after hydration ceased and just before Stacey died, she shed a tear as Dona prayed with her. We believe that was a physical manifestation of God's love, empathy, and compassion. She was leaving us but going to her heavenly Father. (Chapter 21)

14. The prayers of many people were triumphantly and gloriously answered, although not quite the way we'd expected or hoped. God

healed Stacey completely and eternally, not to return to this life but to go to live with Him forever! (Throughout)

15. God preserved our marriage through the most trying and difficult circumstances. (Throughout)

16. God freed me from several oppressions from which I otherwise might not have sought release. (Chapters 23–26)

17. The Lord Himself communicated with me directly with an inner voice and allowed Stacey's "voice" to do the same with comfort and encouragement. (Throughout)

Chronology of
Stacey's Decline

August 25, 1993 (Stacey's accident and surgery):

September 9 (Dr. Clayton's notes on CT scan): "Even with the flap left off to combat swelling and pressure, part of her brain has actually squeezed down through the little hole at the base of her skull and caused the death of some of her brainstem tissue[61] ... inability to clot because of the brain laceration, brain hemorrhage ... devastating intrinsic damage. She would have died (probably the first day) if Dr. Kline hadn't performed *open* head injury. ... She would have stopped breathing and died. ... At this point the only area not involved with abnormalities is the cerebellum. ... pupils fixed, dilated, non-reactive."

September 23: EEG showed no improvement—" ... She remains unresponsive, un-reactive ... pressure spikes in the right occipital region ... potentially epileptogenic activity capable of partial secondarily generalized seizure generation ... diffuse thets and delta slowing ... amplitude suppression over the right hemisphere ["amplitude suppression" refers to a slowing of brain activity. The term suppression is used when little or no electrocerebral activity can be discerned in a tracing. Katie Townley, PA-C 3/26/16.] ... non-purposeful movement of late to noxious stimuli (an injurious stimulus used to evoke a response).[62] Her brainstem evoked potentials, in the context of traumatic encephalopathy continue to indicate a poor prognosis for survival ... no doll's eyes. [The term 'doll's eyes' is used in reference to a test that looks at damage to the brainstem, which controls vital functions such as breathing and heart rate. If a person has positive doll's eyes, that is a better prognostic sign. When the patient's head is turned side-to-side with his eyes open, the eyes will stay fixed on the examiner instead of turning the direction the head is moving. Negative doll's eyes means that the eyes don't stay fixed in the center but turn to look in the direction the head is pulled. This indicates that brainstem function is not intact. KT 3/26/16]"

Notes from other reports on Stacey's progression follow.

September 24: "The entire right hemisphere represents contusion with hemorrhage and edema all probably associated with infarction. ... There's still brain swelling out of the defect, (hole, opening). ... Hydrocephalus presents, ventricles (fluid chambers) are swollen. A large fluid collection on the left frontal region ... residual encephalomalacia[63] from the contusion ... cells are dying, replaced with fluid on left side. ... "

October 5: " ... more brain tissue has degenerated, died. ... Order to remove the ventilator. ... " [Dr. Imber later commented, "If we had decided to remove the ventilator on the first night at Greyson, fourteen days after the accident, she would have not been able to sustain her oxygen levels. She would have stopped breathing and died very soon."]

Late September/mid October: copies of all reports sent to Dr. Zefranye, NY, for review and consult.

Greyson's subsequent notes: "She has no meaningful response to noxious stimuli, painful stimuli. There is no evoke potential, auditory, or otherwise. No meaningful response is there, no evoke potential to noxious stimuli ... some brain tissue left, but none left for cognition ... the cortex-gone ... main frontal and temporal lobes gone. ... Herniation in brainstem ... partial hemorrhage in brainstem ... some infarction in brainstem. ... Because the brainstem controls autonomic responses, the hearing response, temperature response, pupil response—all gone or severely limited."

October 26, 1993 (63 days since the accident): Withdrew hydration and nutrition

October 31, 1993: Stacey's death

NOTES

[1] Hebrews 11:1–16.

[2] *Matthew Henry's Whole Bible Commentary,* Genesis 1: 6–8, http://www. Biblos.com (accessed 2/25/12).

[3] John Newton, Amazing Grace, *http://library.timelesstruths.org/music/ Amazing_Grace*/Cached—Similar (accessed 2/25/12).

[4] *Christian Growth Study Bible,* New International Version, Michigan, Zondervan Corporation, 1997, 514. Print.

[5] Ibid., *Christian Growth Study Bible,* 514. Print.

[6] "Head Injury." *Johns Hopkins Medicine.* The Johns Hopkins University, The Johns Hopkins Hospital, Johns Hopkins Health System. n.d. Web. 13 Mar. 2016.

[7] The term "craniotomy" refers broadly to the surgical removal of a section of the skull in order to access the intracranial compartment. The portion of skull temporarily removed is called a bone flap, and it is replaced to its original position after the operation is completed, typically fastened into place with plates and screws. Craniectomy refers to an operation wherein the bone flap is removed but not replaced.

Hanft, Simon. "Craniotomy." *Medscape.* WebMD, 17 Sept. 2015. Web. 13 Mar. 2016.

[8] **What are the different types of Traumatic Brain Injury?**

Primary brain injury refers to the sudden and profound injury to the brain that is considered to be more or less complete at the time of impact. This happens at the time of the car accident, gunshot wound, or fall.

Secondary brain injury refers to the changes that evolve over a period of hours to days after the primary brain injury. It includes an entire series of steps or stages of cellular, chemical, tissue, or blood vessel changes in the brain that contribute to further destruction of brain tissue.

Penetrating brain injury:
Penetrating, or open head injuries happen when there is a break in the skull, such as when a bullet pierces the brain.

Diffuse axonal injury is the shearing (tearing) of the brain's long connecting nerve fibers (axons) that happens when the brain is injured as it shifts and rotates inside the bony skull. DAI usually causes coma and injury to many different parts of the brain. The changes in the brain are often microscopic and may not be evident on computed tomography (CT scan) or magnetic resonance imaging (MRI) scans. ...

The jarring of the brain against the sides of the skull can cause shearing (tearing) of the internal lining, tissues, and blood vessels leading to internal bleeding, bruising, or swelling of the brain.

Can the brain heal after being injured?
Most studies suggest that once brain cells are destroyed or damaged, for the most part, they do not regenerate. However, recovery after brain injury can take place, especially in younger people, as, in some cases, other areas of the brain make up for the injured tissue. In other cases, the brain learns to reroute information and function around the damaged areas. The exact amount of recovery is not predictable at the time of injury and may be unknown for months or even years. Each brain injury and rate of recovery is unique. Recovery from a severe brain injury often involves a prolonged or lifelong process of treatment and rehabilitation.

What is a coma?
Coma is an altered state of consciousness that may be very deep (unconsciousness) so that no amount of stimulation will cause the patient to respond. It can also be a state of reduced consciousness, so that the patient may move about or respond to pain. Not all patients with brain injury are comatose. The depth of coma and the time a patient spends in a coma varies greatly depending on the location and severity of the brain injury. Some patients emerge from a coma and have a good recovery. Other patients have significant disabilities.

How is coma measured?
Depth of the coma is usually measured in the emergency and intensive care settings using a Glasgow coma scale. The scale (from 3 to

15) evaluates eye opening, verbal response, and motor response. A high score shows a greater amount of consciousness and awareness.

"Traumatic Brain Injury." *Johns Hopkins Medicine.* The Johns Hopkins University, The Johns Hopkins Hospital, Johns Hopkins Health System. n.d. Web. 2 Jan. 2016.

[9] Tracheotomy, also known as a tracheostomy, is an operative procedure that creates a surgical airway in the cervical trachea. It is most often performed in patients who have had difficulty weaning off a ventilator followed by those who have suffered trauma or a catastrophic neurologic insult.

Lindman, Jonathan P. "Tracheostomy." *Medscape.* WebMD, 21 Jan. 2015. Web. 11 Mar. 2016.

[10] **What is an evoked potentials study?**

Evoked potentials studies measure electrical activity in the brain in response to stimulation of sight, sound, or touch. Stimuli delivered to the brain through each of these senses evoke minute electrical signals. These signals travel along the nerves and through the spinal cord to specific regions of the brain and are picked up by electrodes, amplified, and displayed for a doctor to interpret.

Evoked potentials studies involve three major tests that measure response to visual, auditory, and electrical stimuli:

- Visual evoked response (VER) test: This test can diagnose problems with the optic nerves that affect sight. Electrodes are placed along your scalp and the electrical signals are recorded as you watch a checkerboard pattern flash for several minutes on a screen.
- Brainstem auditory evoked response (BAER) test: This test can diagnose hearing ability and can point to possible brainstem tumors or multiple sclerosis. Electrodes are placed on your scalp and earlobes and auditory stimuli, such as clicking noises and tones, are delivered to one ear.
- Somatosensory evoked response (SSER) test: This test can detect problems with the spinal cord as well as numbness and weakness of the extremities. For this test, electrodes are attached to your wrist, the back of your knee, or other locations. A mild electrical stimulus is applied through the electrodes. Electrodes on your scalp then determine the amount of time it takes for the current to travel along the nerves to the brain.

"Evoked Potentials Studies." *Johns Hopkins Medicine.* The Johns Hopkins University, The Johns Hopkins Hospital, Johns Hopkins Health System. n.d. Web. 15 Mar. 2016.

[11] Decompressive craniectomy (DC) is a surgical procedure used to relieve severely increased intracranial pressure (ICP) by removing a portion of the skull. Following DC, the brain expands through the skull defect created by DC, resulting in transcalvarial herniation (TCH).

Liao CC, Tsai YH, Chen YL, Huang KC, Chiang IJ, Wong JM, and Xiao F. "Transcalvarial brain herniation volume after decompressive craniectomy is the difference between two spherical caps." *PubMed.* US National Library of Medicine National Institutes of Health. Epub 30 Dec. 2014. Web. 15 Mar. 2016.

[12] Elevated intracranial pressure (ICP) is seen in head trauma, hydrocephalus, intracranial tumors, hepatic encephalopathy, and cerebral edema. Intractable elevated ICP can lead to death or devastating neurological damage either by reducing cerebral perfusion pressure (CPP) and causing cerebral ischemia or by compressing and causing herniation of the brainstem or other vital structures. Prompt recognition is crucial in order to intervene appropriately.

Intractable high ICP is the most common "terminal event" leading to death in neurosurgical patients. The association between the severity of intracranial hypertension and poor outcome after severe head injury is well recognized. Outcomes tend to be good in patients with normal ICP, whereas those with elevated ICP are much more likely to have an unfavorable outcome. Elevated ICP carries a mortality rate of around 20 percent.

Gupta, Gaurav, MD; "Intracranial Pressure Monitoring." *Medscape.* WebMD, 17 Sept. 2015. Web. 15 Mar. 2016.

[13] MOTOR RESPONSES The motor examination in a stuporous or comatose patient is, of necessity, quite different from the patient who is awake and cooperative. Rather than testing power in specific muscles, it is focused on assessing the overall responsiveness of the patient (as measured by motor response), the motor tone, and reflexes, and identifying abnormal motor patterns, such as hemiplegia or abnormal posturing. ... Responses are graded as appropriate, inappropriate, or no response. An appropriate response is one that attempts to escape the stimulus, such as pushing the stimulus away or attempting to avoid the stimulus. ... Flexor posturing of the upper extremities and extension of the lower extremities corresponds to the pattern of movement also called decorticate

posturing. ... Even more ominous is the presence of extensor posturing of both the upper and lower extremities, often called decerebrate posturing.

The arms are held in adduction and extension with the wrists fully pronated. Some patients assume an opisthotonic posture, with teeth clenched and arching of the spine. ... It represents a more severe finding than decorticate posturing; for example, in the Jennett and Teasdale series, only 10 percent of comatose patients with head injury who demonstrated decerebrate posturing recovered.

Plum, Fred, and Jerome B. Posner. *Plum and Posner's Diagnosis of Stupor and Coma.* 4th ed., Oxford, New York: Oxford Press, 2007. 72–75. Print.

[14] Infarction: a condition in which the blood supply to an area of tissue is blocked and the tissue dies.

Oxford Learner's Dictionary; 2016 Oxford University Press. n.d. Web. 16 Mar. 2016.

[15] What is hydrocephalus?

Hydrocephalus is a condition characterized by an abnormal accumulation of cerebrospinal fluid (CSF) within the ventricles of the brain. CSF surrounds the brain and spinal cord. When the circulatory path of the CSF is blocked, fluid begins to accumulate, causing the ventricles to enlarge and the pressure inside the head to increase, resulting in hydrocephalus. ... There is another form of hydrocephalus that does not fit exactly into the categories mentioned above and primarily affect adults: hydrocephalus ex-vacuo. Hydrocephalus ex-vacuo occurs when stroke, degenerative diseases like Alzheimer's disease or other dementias or traumatic injury cause damage to the brain. In these cases, brain tissue may actually shrink.

"Hydrocephalus." *Johns Hopkins Medicine.* The Johns Hopkins University, The Johns Hopkins Hospital, Johns Hopkins Health System. n.d. Web. 15 Mar. 2016.

[16] Plum, Fred, and Jerome B. Posner. Plum and Posner's Diagnosis of Stupor and Coma. 4th ed., Oxford, New York: Oxford Press, 2007. 95–102. Print.

[17] Ibid, Plum and Posner, 357–360.

[18] Ibid, Plum and Posner, 65.

[19] Ibid, Plum and Posner, 65–68.

[20] Plum, Fred, and Jerome B. Posner. *Diagnosis of Stupor and Coma.* 2nd ed. Contemporary Neurology Series. Philadelphia: F.A. Davis Company, Seventh Printing 1976. 224–239. Print.

[21] Ibid, Plum and Posner, 224–225.

[22] Ibid, Plum and Posner, 224–225.

[23] Ibid, Plum and Posner, 235.

[24] Eareckson Tada, Joni. *A Lifetime of Wisdom.* Grand Rapids, Michigan: Zondervan, 2009. 194. Print.

[25] Chambers, Oswald. *My Utmost for His Highest.* Tennessee: Oswald Chambers Publications Association, Ltd, 1992. December 13. Print.

[26] Dillard, Annie. *Pilgrim at Tinker Creek.* New York: Harper & Row Publishers, First Perennial Library Edition, 1985. 33. Print.

[27] As a weaned child—viz. not one that is only just begun to be weaned, but an actually weaned child (גמל, cognate גמר eta, to bring to an end, more particularly to bring suckling to an end, to wean)—lies upon its mother without crying impatiently and craving for its mother's breast but contented with the fact that it has its mother—like such a weaned child is his soul upon him, i.e., in relation to his Ego (which is conceived of in עלי as having the soul upon itself, cf. Psalm 42:7. Jeremiah 8:18. Psychology, S. 151f, tr. p. 180): his soul, which is by nature restless and craving, is stilled. It does not long after earthly enjoyment and earthly good that God should give these to it, but it is satisfied in the fellowship of God, it finds full satisfaction in Him, it is satisfied (satiated) in Him.

Keil and Delietsch. *Biblical Commentary on the Old Testament: Psalm 131.* Bible Hub. n.d. Web. 13 Mar. 2016.

[28] Ibid, Keil and Delietsch, Psalm 131.

[29] Mennonite Mutual Aid. *Life Choices, Guidelines for Creating Your Advance Medical Directives.* Goshen, Indiana: Mennonite Mutual Aid, c. 1992, 1993. 10. Print.

[30] In 1982 Fred Plum and Jerome B. Posner defined the clinical criteria for diagnosis of a coma: Absence of sleep/wake cycles on EEG. Continuous eye closure, no evidence of awareness of self or environment, incapable of interacting with others, no purposeful motor activity, no behavioral response to command, no evidence of language comprehension or expression, inability to discretely localize noxious stimuli.

Plum, Fred, and Jerome B. Posner. *Plum and Posner's Diagnosis of Stupor and Coma.* 4th ed., Oxford, New York: Oxford Press, 2007. 7. Print.

[31] Ibid. Plum and Posner, 7.

[32] Sommers, Ernest. Personal interview. 25 Jan. 2011.

[33] See Addendum One.

[34] Blackaby, Henry, Richard Blackaby, and Claude King. *Experiencing God.* Nashville, Tennessee: B & H Publishing Group, 2008. 190. Print.

[35] Chambers, Oswald. *My Utmost for His Highest.* Tennessee: Oswald Chambers Publications Association, Ltd, 1992. February 18. Print.

[36] Blackaby, Henry, Richard Blackaby, and Claude King. *Experiencing God.* Nashville, Tennessee: B & H Publishing Group, 2008. 209. Print.

[37] Chambers, Oswald. *My Utmost for His Highest.* Uhrichsville, Ohio: Barbour Publishing, 1994. February 22. Print.

[38] Mains, David, Steve Bell, Dennis Clements, Jennifer Knaak, Daniel Lupton, Marian Oliver, and Randy Petersen. *Daring to Dream Again.* Wheaton, Illinois: The Chapel of the Air Inc., 1993. 7. Print.

[39] Voskamp, Ann. *One Thousand Gifts.* Grand Rapids, Michigan: Zondervan, 2010. 220–221. Print.

[40] Moore, Beth. *Believing God.* Nashville, Tennessee: LifeWay Press, 2004. 166. Print.

[41] James, John W., and Russell Friedman. *The Grief Recovery Handbook.* 20th Anniversary Expanded ed. New York: Harper-Collins Publishers, 2009. 63–65. Print.

[42] Moore, Beth. *Believing God.* Nashville, Tennessee: LifeWay Press, 2004. Print.

[43] Unknown.

[44] "Nigel Mumford to Lead Healing Service at Our Savior." Gideon's Trumpet, Vol. 2006, Issue 1. Lebanon Springs, New York. 19 Feb. 2006. 8–9. Print.

[45] Jeffress, Robert. *Grace Gone Wild.* Colorado Springs, Colorado: Waterbrook Press, 2005. 107–108. Print.

[46] James, John W., and Russell Friedman. *The Grief Recovery Handbook.* 20th Anniversary Expanded ed. New York: Harper-Collins Publishers, 2009. 145–146. Print.

[47] McGee, Robert S. *The Search for Significance*. Houston, Texas: Rapha Publishing, 1990. 61. Print.

[48] Ibid, McGee, 289–290.

[49] Thomas, Angela. *Do You Think I'm Beautiful?* Nashville, Tennessee: Thomas Nelson Publishers, 2003. 170. Print.

[50] Jackson, Kit. "The Way of Pain." Personal Testimony. See Addendum Two.

[51] Thomas, Angela. *Do You Think I'm Beautiful?* Nashville, Tennessee: Thomas Nelson Publishers, 2003. 170. Print.

[52] Julian of Norwich. *A Revelation of Love*. Ed. & trans. John Skinner. New York/London: Image Books/Doubleday, 1996. 149–151. Print.

[53] Yancey, Philip. *Disappointment with God*. New York: HarperPaperbacks, A Division of HarperCollinsPublishers, 1988. 236. Print.

[54] See Addendum Three.

[55] Moore, Beth. *Believing God*. Nashville, Tennessee: LifeWay Press, 2004. 191. Print.

[56] Evans, Tony. *Dry Bones Dancing*. Colorado Springs, Colorado: Multnomah Books, 2005. 121–122. Print.

[57] Luke 22:20

[58] "The Beautiful Sayings of Saint Bonventure, 1221–1274," *A Christian Pilgrimage*, 11 July 2011. Web. 8 March 2012.

[59] Ibid, Bonventure.

[60] Medwick, Cathleen. *Teresa of Avila, The Progress of a Soul*. New York: Doubleday, a division of Random House, Inc., 1999. First Image books Edition: February 2001. xvii. Print.

[61] Plum, Fred, and Jerome B. Posner. *Plum and Posner's Diagnosis of Stupor and Coma*. 4th ed., Oxford, New York: Oxford Press, 2007. 100–103. Print.

[62] Ibid, Plum and Posner, 65–68.

[63] Encephalomalacia: softening of the brain; infarction of brain tissue, usually caused by vascular insufficiency.
"Encephalomalacia." *Stedman's Medical Dictionary*. 23rd ed. Baltimore, Maryland: Williams & Wilkins, December 1979. Print.

ACKNOWLEDGMENTS

To these I owe a great debt of gratitude:

The editors: Marsha Hubler, Kate, Jean Marie, Mary Ann, Megan Rongone. Oh my, the "that"s we removed, the commas that came and went, and the myriad of words we sorted through to find the best way to say what needed to be said.

The authors from the writers' groups who critiqued my work, continued to encourage me, and made me a better writer. Thanks Sue Fairchild, Roberta Brosius, Marsha Hubler, and so many others.

Brenda Hendrix, Angela Schans, Kasey, and Carrie: Will I ever get this social media stuff?

Dr I. and Dr. K.: You know who you are. My family and I know who you are—two of the most dedicated physicians ever. Thanks for your review of Stacey's records and for your critique of the medical portion of this work. Most of all, thanks for taking care of all of us.

The shepherd-pastors: The Lord honors your good work on behalf of His beloved. I thank God for your spiritual support throughout the journey.

Kate: How can I say thanks for hour upon hour, month after month of tirelessly sitting beside me to make this book the best it could be? You saw me through to the end. Thank you for being part of this and part of my life. God bless you.

Dona: You have stuck by me since grade school. You helped me paint the pictures that tell this story. You are a gifted artist. Thank you, my friend.

To each of my seven brothers and sisters and their families: You prayed us through. Steven, you faithfully read the Scriptures to her. Bonny, you took care of my Stacey when I could not be there for her. I am forever thankful for who you are and how you loved Stacey and love me. Mary Ann, you gave generously, from computer to printer to the mountain house where we corralled ourselves and travailed through the journey.

Devoted friends and Bible study women, too numerous to list, who have upheld me throughout the whole process.

My husband and children, without whom I would have given up a long time ago—and my precious grandchildren who made me laugh through my tears.

Finally, thanks be to God the Father and our Lord Jesus Christ who causes all things to work together for good and for His glory. May He be praised forever.